AMERICAN LIBRARY PIONEERS
Emily Miller Danton
Editor

VII

CHARLES COFFIN JEWETT

AMERICAN LIBRARY PIONEERS

CHARLES COFFIN JEWETT

BY

Joseph A. Borome

CHICAGO

AMERICAN LIBRARY ASSOCIATION

1951

For HELEN E. HAINES, *inspiring teacher and friend*

Preface

MORE THAN eighty years have passed since Charles Coffin Jewett, the most renowned American librarian of his time, breathed his last. His had been an honored career. In 1841, at the age of twenty-five, he had been appointed to the librarianship of Brown University; seven years later he had resigned in order to take charge of the library affairs of the newly established Smithsonian Institution in Washington. In 1854 he had been summarily dismissed, with much attendant furor, and the following year had returned to his native New England where he entered the service of the Boston Public Library. From 1858 until his death in 1868 he was its distinguished superintendent. A man of imagination and enthusiasm, limitless energy, and singular originality, he strove during the greater part of his life to solve many of the challenging problems of his day singlehandedly and by means of projects fashioned on a large scale. These endeavors related to bibliography, cataloging, exchanges, the circulation of books, and cooperative efforts among librarians. Within the span of some thirty years he pushed a majority of his ambitious projects to completion and made an impressive number of substantial contributions to librarianship. For years after Jewett's death, William F. Poole, William I. Fletcher, and other librarians, who themselves helped to lay the groundwork for the modern library movement, continued to acknowledge a lasting debt to his pioneer efforts and to extol his accomplishments. Yet, ironically, Jewett is more often remembered today because of one of his failures — the famed stereotyping scheme.

Save for a not-too-lengthy article by Reuben Aldridge Guild in the *Library Journal* of 1887, there exists no detailed record of the life and labors of this assiduous toiler in the vineyard of librarianship. This volume, which does not purport to be exhaustive, is offered as an attempt to remedy that deficiency.

For reading parts, or the entire draft of this work and giving fully of their criticism, I am indebted to Helen E. Haines; Harry M. Lydenberg; Dr. Jesse H. Shera, assistant professor, University of Chicago Graduate Library School; Milton E. Lord, director, Boston Public Library; Dr. Sidney H. Ditzion, assistant librarian, College of the City of New York Library; Zoltán Haraszti, keeper of rare books, Boston Public Library; Dr. Maurice F. Tauber, professor, Columbia University School of Library Service; David C. Mearns, assistant librarian, Library of Congress; and Merton L. Reichler. I wish also to thank Dr. Alexander Wetmore, secretary of the Smithsonian Institution, for having the manuscript examined by members of his staff; the Reverend Richard D. Pierce, associate librarian, Andover Newton Theological Library, for supplying material on Jewett as a student there; Amos E. Jewett for furnishing information on the Jewett family and a copy of Charles Jewett's oration of 1855, and for granting permission to publish a letter of Jewett's in his possession; Penelope B. Noyes for permitting the use of the Justin Winsor papers in her possession; Everett O. Fontaine, chief of the Publishing Department of the American Library Association, for providing a copy of George B. Utley's manuscript on the 1853 Librarians' Conference; James I. Wyer, for making available a bibliography of materials he had compiled on Jewett; Elizabeth Brockunier, for securing copies of a portrait and signature of Jewett; and the Department of State for ferreting out a copy of Jewett's 1843 passport.

Throughout the text, citations have been given only to manuscript papers; the secondary materials from which statements are drawn are listed in the bibliographical notes at the conclusion of the work. The opinions expressed and any errors of fact are my own responsibility.

I have been allowed, by courtesy of the trustees of the Public Library of the City of Boston, as well as the administrations of the following libraries, to quote from manuscripts in their possession: American Antiquarian Society Library, Brown University Library, Harvard University Library, Johns Hopkins University Library, Library of Congress, Massachusetts Historical Society Library, New York Public Library. The members of their staffs, and the staff of the Columbia University Libraries, have placed me under obligation by their courteous services. The aid of my wife, Flora Anne Borome, in ways too numerous to describe, is hereby gratefully acknowledged.

Joseph Borome

June 5, 1950

Contents

CHARLES COFFIN JEWETT

I

Youth and Early Manhood

In the year 1638 Deacon Maximilian and Joseph, two sons of Edward Jewett, an English clothier of Bradford, the West Riding of Yorkshire, left their native land to escape the heavy hand of Archbishop Laud's Anglican tyranny. Landing in Boston, they passed the winter there and the following year settled on the town site of Rowley, Massachusetts.

Paul, of the sixth generation of American Jewetts, was born in Rowley on April 26, 1780. He grew up in a family of eight brothers and sisters, all watched over by a father who, near the close of his life in 1828, had almost attained the age of ninety and was known as "the oldest man in town." In his late teens Paul attended Rhode Island College, later Brown University, earning his degree in 1802. The college authorities appointed him a tutor, and for three years, from 1806 to 1809, he held that position. When a period of competent service finally entitled him to promotion and they offered him a professorship, he declined it, for he had decided that he preferred the ministry to pedagogy. Accordingly, he severed his connection with the college and set about preparing himself for his chosen calling. In 1812, the year "Mr. Madison's war" (as it was popularly known in New England) began, he was engaged to preach at

3

the Congregational Church in Lebanon, Maine. On September 1, 1813, he married Eleanor Masury Punchard in Salem, Massachusetts. She had been born there on May 21, 1792, the daughter of John and Kezia Punchard. The young couple moved to Lebanon, where, in 1814, Paul Jewett was "ordained to the Pastoral care of the church."

For a time all went well. A more general interest in religion developed in the town, and the church was considerably enlarged. The minister enjoyed the esteem of his congregation. His family life appears to have been happy and contented, and as the years passed the quiet of his dwelling was broken by the carefree laughter of children. In 1814 a son, John Punchard — destined to achieve fame as the publisher of *Uncle Tom's Cabin*— was born. On August 12, 1816, Eleanor presented Paul with another son, Charles Coffin. In 1818 George Baker was born.

Not long after, "difficulties arose" in church affairs and the Reverend Jewett requested a dismissal. Heeding the advice of a church council, he withdrew from office in October, 1819, and returned to Salem with his family. On October 2, 1822, his wife died, and four years later his son, Henry Paul, who had been born in 1820. In Scituate, Massachusetts on May 24, 1827, he wed the widowed Grace Torrey Thaxter, by whom he later had one girl and two boys who lived to maturity. A retiring man of much ability and refined tastes, he found little permanence in positions. What seems to have been a rather unsettled clerical life—he ministered thereafter to churches in Scituate, Carver, Topsfield, and Hamil-

4

ton — ended suddenly, on May 15, 1840, with an attack of apoplexy.

Charles Coffin Jewett passed his childhood in Salem. In due course he entered the Latin School, graduating in 1831. He promptly matriculated at Dartmouth College, but hardly a year had passed before he transferred to his father's alma mater, from which he graduated, the youngest member of his class, in 1835. He obtained the position of "preceptor" at the Uxbridge (Massachusetts) Academy, where he remained until a desire for the work of the ministry overwhelmed him and he resolved to acquire theological training. In the fall of 1837 he was admitted to Andover Seminary.

The missionary spirit was then rife among a majority of American religious denominations. As early as 1820 New England missionaries had landed in Hawaii. The decade after had seen several set out for China and men like Jason Lee and Marcus Whitman wend their way to Oregon for work among the Indians. When Charles entered the seminary many Andover men were going forth as missionaries, and his own predilection for similar endeavor was strong.

For three years he labored over the subject matter of "Natural Theology," "Evidences of Revelation," "Principles of Hermeneutics," "Homiletics," and other required courses, giving especial attention to philology and "Oriental languages and Eastern antiquities." The latter subjects soon proved so congenial to his interests, and he became so proficient in them — a proficiency that made a lasting impression upon Professors Justin Edwards and Moses Stuart who instructed him — that his intention to

5

devote himself to missionary work underwent modification.[1] He determined, once he had his degree in hand, to visit Palestine and Asia, "partly for missionary purposes, but mainly for extensive researches in Biblical antiquities." A number of renowned scholars encouraged him in this purpose. In 1840 Charles delivered a graduation address "The Utility of the Arabic Language in the Interpretation of the Old Testament," which was penned in so elegant a style that it evoked considerable favorable comment. Soon after, he made ready for his journey to the Orient. He booked passage on a certain vessel; but when it departed he was not aboard, for the letter informing him of its sailing time, having been incorrectly addressed, had reached him too late.

In the spring of 1841 he assumed the office of principal of Day's Academy in Wrentham, Massachusetts. Here he met the assistant who became his lifelong friend and admirer, Reuben Aldridge Guild. Principal Jewett had been in service but a few months before he resigned to accept a call from Brown University to take charge of its library.

On the basis of inclination and experience he was well qualified for his new position. As a youth he had been very fond of books and reading. In college he and a fellow student, William Lawton Brown, had classified and cataloged the books belonging to the Philermenian, one of the three student societies of the day, and had arranged them in cases in the society's room. At Andover

[1]He became a member of the Society of Inquiry, a missionary study club, as did most of the student body; but he did not join the Brethren, the society of students committed to the mission field. (Rev. Richard D. Pierce to writer, October 4, 1945).

he had not been long upon his course of study before his continued interest in the preparation and arrangement for use of books in libraries, and in bibliography, singled him out of the student body and attracted the attention of Oliver Alden Taylor, the librarian, who was then preparing a catalog of the library. He invited Jewett to assist him, and in 1838 brought out the volume which German librarians were long to regard as a model, the *Catalogue of the Library of the Theol. Seminary*. In this period the library was in the care of one of the trustees or professors, with one of the students as acting librarian. Because of his aid to Taylor, Jewett was appointed librarian, a position he held for more than a year, while pursuing his regular study program. In addition to an acquaintance with library economy, experience in library work, and training in bibliography, Jewett had, by 1841, a distinct scholarly bent and a knowledge of the literature of modern languages greatly increased since college days. Before the university offered him the headship of the Brown library, the full measure of these qualifications had been taken.

As he entered upon his Providence duties in the fall of 1841, Jewett probably recalled the library facilities during his student days. The library then was in "an apartment in University Hall, crowded to excess, unsightly, and wholly unsuited for the purpose to which from necessity it was devoted." There, in a small, low-studded room without proper ventilation, some nine thousand ill-selected volumes that overflowed the shelves were kept in a state of darkness sufficient to hide their poor physical condition. Indeed, not a few were "ragged and un-

7

sightly." All were classified, after the manner of Brunet, into five grand divisions of form: folios, quartos, octavos, duodecimos, and "other mos." Circulation rules were based upon a rigid adherence to classification. Thus, a student might retain a folio volume for four weeks and two duodecimos for two.

Though a ruling of the corporation in 1834 had provided that the librarian be in attendance daily from ten in the morning until noon during the semester, the library was open to students only three days a week, each day for one hour. Few New England colleges then knew such liberality. Some twenty years later the libraries of Colby and Wesleyan were open but one half hour twice a week and that of Amherst only once a week. In a day when the predominant library policy was one of the accumulation and preservation of books, it was not deemed necessary to make collections accessible for a great many hours. Moreover, the undergraduates, for whom textbooks were supposed to suffice, were to avail themselves of the allotted time primarily to take and return books, not to use them within the library. The privilege of reading in the Brown library was extended to graduate students, donors, and other classes of individuals, but the undergraduates were warned that they might not pass into the library room beyond the librarian's table, nor might they "while receiving books . . . take down any book from the shelves without special permission of the Librarian."

These conditions had not long escaped the attention of Brown's President Wayland. A firm believer in the value of libraries, private and public, that eminent educator had noted early in his presidency, which began in 1827, that the students rarely made use of the resources of the library and also that it furnished little assistance to occasional visiting scholars. In 1831, owing largely to his efforts, measures were taken to raise by subscription $25,000 to be used for "the purchase of books for the library and apparatus for the philosophical and chemical departments." More than $19,000 was obtained, lent at interest until it had increased to $25,000, and then invested as a permanent fund. The interest on the "Library Fund," as it was known, amounted to about $500 a year. After 1839, when the first dividend fell due, it was drawn upon annually for the purchase of books.

With funds assured for book purchase, it was imperative that the library have new and more spacious quarters. A chapel was also needed. At a suggestion from Wayland, Nicholas Brown, the philanthropist who was the university's chief benefactor, offered to erect a building to house both library and chapel—an architectural arrangement by no means infrequent at the time. On February 4, 1835, Manning Hall was dedicated with impressive ceremonies which Jewett, of the senior class, witnessed. The library occupied the lower floor of the edifice. It measured sixty-four feet in length and thirty-eight in width. Through the center of the room, thirteen feet high, ran parallel rows of fluted Grecian columns, separated by an aisle in which stood the librarian's table. From each column bookshelves extended to the walls to form twelve alcoves.

What of the librarian? Because of the small collections and the slight use made of them, the colleges of the period, with rare exceptions, did not view as essential the employment of a librarian to devote his entire attention to the library. Consequently, there arose in most institutions the obvious and economical practice of joining library duties with pedagogical ones. So it was at Brown. During Jewett's student days, Horatio Gates Bowen, professor of natural history, performed the double service. When he retired in 1840, after sixteen years of faithful labor, Professor William Gammell was named to the position as acting librarian. He soon found himself hard put to it to continue in both offices, for the library collection was growing and the responsibilities of its charge increasing; and he resigned. Professor Alexis Caswell, his successor, quickly came to the same conclusion. At this juncture, on October 2, 1841, the library committee resolved that Jewett be appointed full-time librarian at an annual salary of $600, and be specifically directed to compile a catalog of the library. On October 11 he took up his tasks. '

One of his first acts was to devise an arrangement of books that would prove practical for users of the library. The shelves, designed to accommodate thirty thousand volumes, were numbered, and the books, sorted according to size and, where convenient, according to subject matter, were assigned fixed positions upon them. The shelf location number was stamped on the back of each volume. Shelf-listing and cataloging then followed. These procedures having been established, Jewett turned to the matter of the catalog.

There had been two catalogs of the library, one in 1791 containing 2173 volumes, the other in 1826 showing

5818. The latter was a list of authors entered alphabetically under subjects. Many advances had since been made in the compilation of catalogs, and Jewett, conversant with the newer techniques of America and Europe, set out to employ them. For almost two years he pegged away at the catalog. On August 12, 1843, he dated his preface which contained a history of the library, a statement of the principles he had followed in constructing the catalog, and a list of the rules of the library. That fall the result of his painstaking labors, the *Catalogue of the Library of Brown University,* came from the press.

This volume of 576 pages was divided into two parts. The first, following Taylor's Andover plan, listed all the works in the library alphabetically by author. Beneath each author's name appeared, first, his complete works, then single titles alphabetically, and, lastly, biographies written by others. Anonymous works were entered, either under the first important word of their titles or under the subjects to which they were most closely related, or were grouped, as were a considerable number, under such headings as "Great Britain" and "United States." Two significant features of the first portion of the *Catalogue* were the frequent biographical notices of authors, particularly of American writers, and the occasional bibliographical notes on important items. The second part, based chiefly upon the plan of the catalog of the Signet Library, of Edinburgh, was a very full subject index — alphabetical and classified — with many cross references.

The *Catalogue* was immediately recognized as an outstanding and unique work and elicited widespread praise and lengthy commendatory notices in several periodicals of the day, including the *North American Review*. Printed college library catalogs were not, to be sure, unknown. Bowdoin had printed one in 1819 (120 pages), Harvard in 1830-1831 (4 volumes), Trinity in 1832 (24 pages), and Wesleyan in 1837 (50 pages). All these were brief, title-a-line compilations. The importance of Jewett's production derived from its bipartite design, alphabetical arrangement, abundant cross references, and minuteness of detail. Even so, it did not fully conform to his original plan, which had called for biographical notices for all authors, more detailed "registrations," and more numerous "cross references from author to author & book to book."[2] These features he had had to modify toward the end so as to hurry the work along and not exceed the university appropriation.

Hardly had the *Catalogue* appeared before a new department of instruction was established by the university, and Jewett was named professor of modern languages and literature. He would continue to hold the librarianship — the university, now that the catalog had been completed, having reverted to the time-honored dual-position practice. That he might more ably fill his new office he was granted a leave of absence to visit Europe where he was to familarize himself with the literature of the modern languages, purchase books for the Brown library, make the acquaintance of noted librarians, and investigate library methods.

[2]C. C. Jewett to Samuel Foster Haven, January 24, 1850, Correspondence Files, American Antiquarian Society.

While preparing to depart, he was consulted by John Carter Brown, the youngest son of Nicholas Brown and a noted bibliophile, who, having the utmost confidence in his ability and a strong desire to purchase works in the French language for the university, asked Jewett to collect for him information "in reference to the book trade in France." Jewett readily consented to do so, added this charge to his others, turned the library over to the Reverend Dr. Robinson Potter Dunn, the assistant librarian, and sailed for Europe.

He passed his first three months in Paris, delving into the book resources of the city, and sent John Carter Brown a report of his findings. The latter, impressed with the survey, at once forwarded 5000 francs to be spent at Jewett's discretion on such works as might best constitute the foundation of a French library. During most of the three following months Jewett devoted himself to this endeavor. The success of his efforts and his shrewd buying netted the university 89 folios, 735 octavos, 480 smaller-sized volumes, and 20 maps.

His travels led him next to Germany. Here, at the suggestion of a friend who was an officer in the Royal Guards, he addressed a written request to the King of Prussia for a history of the Seven Years' War published by the Prussian Military Staff, a work that could not be procured at the shops, but only by application to the King. His Majesty was pleased to present the history, and what became perhaps the only American copy of this valuable exposition of the role of Frederick the Great in that struggle was later received by Brown University through the hands of Henry Wheaton, the American min-

ister at Berlin. The Brown library committee dispatched
£200 sterling for purchases in Germany and Italy, an
amount further increased by John Carter Brown, who
sent 4000 francs for German works and, later, 6000 francs
for Italian and Latin publications. Brown especially
asked that Jewett acquire, among his Italian purchases,
"some on the fine arts" of which the library was "lam-
entably barren." While in Italy Jewett obtained some
objets d'art and antiques, among them several small
Etruscan vases. He returned to Paris in the summer of
1845. There he found a draft from the library committee
for 3000 francs. Of this sum he expended 1200 francs
upon the purchase of a telescope, and the remainder on
books, a goodly part of them in the field of science.

Jewett then departed for England where for six months
he repeated his course upon the Continent: he visited
libraries and librarians, never failing to study their
methods of constructing catalogs; he called upon book
publishers and their agents, met men of letters, and
attended book sales and auctions. His itinerary included
Oxford and Cambridge that he might look into their
libraries' workings and collections. For a period he was
almost a daily frequenter of the British Museum, during
which time he examined the management of its library
thoroughly and formed an abiding friendship with the
keeper of printed books (and later principal librarian),
Anthony Panizzi. During Jewett's absence friends of
Brown University had subscribed almost $5000 to remedy
the library's deficiencies in standard English works.
When this sum was made available to him Jewett continued his sedulous book buying, selecting among the

works in the English language a complete set of Hansard's *Parliamentary Debates*. Almost as if the benefactors of the University had not been generous enough, he received £100 from Moses B. Ives for the purchase of such volumes as he desired to select.

Before embarking for America, he visited Rowley, in Yorkshire, whence it was believed that the ancestors of the Jewetts in America had come. His hopes of finding some written account of the family at the church were dashed to the ground by the discovery that its records prior to 1705 had been destroyed and that the local pastor could furnish no information. (Not until 1854 would it be learned that the Jewetts had derived from Bradford).

In December, 1845, Jewett returned to the United States, and before long laid a report of his activities before the library committee. Through his exertions, 7021 books had been acquired, many at provincial sales, but most at auctions in Paris, Rome, Leipzig, Frankfort, and Berlin, and at an average price of $1.20 a volume — a price which included binding and "other expenses of every kind up to the time of shipping." This performance was to remain unequaled for more than a decade, or until Joseph Green Cogswell, journeying through Europe, would purchase for the Astor library sixty thousand volumes, from the vast collections thrown upon the market by the political disturbances of the late forties, at a cost of sixty-three thousand dollars. By the end of 1845 the Brown library, which on January 1, 1843, contained 10,235 volumes, possessed upwards of twenty thousand. Because of the generosity of donors and the judicious selecting by Jewett, it now had a large number of sets of French, Italian, Latin, German, and English classics, several contemporary philosophical, historical and scientific works, many complete series, such as the *Allgemeine Literatur-Zeitung* (134 volumes), and a collection of Shakespeariana amounting to 196 volumes.

His sojourn concluded, Professor Jewett assumed his full responsibilities. Doubtless he conveyed an impression of boundless energy as he hurried across the campus. In the classroom students beheld a dark-complexioned man of average height (five feet, seven inches) and perhaps of medium build, with glossy black hair, a full face, an aquiline nose, and, beneath a high forehead, a pair of deep-set gray eyes, unusually kind in expression. If he appeared assured and a little proud in bearing, there was much in his situation to account for these outward manifestations of self-confidence. At the age of twenty-nine he held not only the librarianship of one of the noted New England institutions of learning, but a newly created chair in one of its expanding departments of instruction.

Besides his experience as a librarian and his familiarity with the literature of the modern languages, he brought to bear the riper knowledge acquired during more than two years of study, first-hand observation, and travel abroad. Before long his success as a teacher rivaled his fame as a librarian. He had a faculty readily appreciated by the undergraduates, the instinctive ability to impart knowledge without condescension, and this was admirably complemented by a deep sense of sympathy with the problems of individual students. These characteristics, combined with warm human qualities, a pleasing voice, a ready smile, and a kind manner, formed strong bonds of affection between himself and those who sat at his feet. It was not without reason that James B. Angell, later president of the University of Michigan, could recall some sixty years after his sophomore days that Jewett, who instructed him in French, "was greatly beloved by the students."

The fortunes of the library advanced under Jewett's guidance, and the collection continued to increase. In 1846, when the passage of the Walker tariff with its free-trade tint was being urged in Congress, he prepared a pamphlet, *Facts and Considerations Relative to Duties on Books,* wherein he urged the Brown library committee to "immediate and energetic efforts" to prevent an increase in the current duties, and marshaled abundant arguments on the merits of repealing all duties levied on foreign books imported by libraries of the United States. On July 30 President James K. Polk signed the tariff bill. Eleven days later the President gave his approval to an act of Congress, the provisions of which had been the subject of much dispute and debate and were destined to alter the course of Jewett's life.

II

Disposition of a Will

On June 27, 1829, James Smithson, illegitimate son of
the Duke of Northumberland and a British chemist of
note, died in Genoa, Italy. His will, when read, was
found to contain a bequest to an old servant and a provision that a nephew, Henry James Hungerford, might
enjoy the income from his property so long as the latter
should live. In the event of the death of Hungerford
without children, however, the entire estate was to be
presented to the government of the United States, "to
found at Washington, under the name of the Smithsonian
Institution, an establishment for the increase and diffusion of knowledge among men." Smithson's motives for
favoring the United States and not Great Britain have
never been fully determined, but they appear to stem in
part from the fact that during his lifetime he smarted
from the snubs of members of English society who, aware
of the circumstances of his birth, kept him outside the
pale of recognition.

In 1835 Smithson's nephew died, and the United States
legation in London was informed that the estate, valued
at about half a million dollars, was in the possession of
the court of chancery. These tidings were relayed to
Congress by President Andrew Jackson who, although
he took a broad view of the powers of his office, felt he

18

did not have the authority to accept the gift. The matter was referred to committees in both houses. Several members of the Senate, among them John C. Calhoun and other strict constructionists, protested against acceptance, Calhoun, indeed, stating that in his opinion it was beneath the national dignity to receive a present from a foreigner. In the House, where opposition also developed, sat John Quincy Adams who, when president of the United States, had urged federal sponsorship of the arts and sciences. The enormous possibilities of Smithson's gift opened before his eyes, and he brought such eloquence and political pressure to bear where they would do the most good that his enlightened opinions prevailed. A bill authorizing the prosecution of the claim passed the House and the Senate, and was signed by President Jackson in July, 1836. Richard Rush hastened to England to enter a suit in the name of the president. Within two years the decision had been rendered, and over the ocean sped the packet "Mediator" transporting £104,960 in gold sovereigns, to be deposited in the federal mint at Philadelphia and recoined into American money.

In 1838, by order of President Martin Van Buren, the Secretary of State addressed letters to a number of distinguished men of the country, soliciting advice on how the $508,314.46 might best be spent. The answers were diverse indeed. John Quincy Adams recommended the establishment of a national observatory, Thomas Cooper and Francis Wayland the founding of a national university, and Richard Rush an agricultural museum and experiment station. Some wished to see the construction of an art gallery, others proposed a program of lectures, and still others suggested the founding of a library. From time to time the subject evoked discussion in Congress. During the Twenty-Sixth Congress (1839-1841) a bill was introduced looking to the creation, with the larger portion of the sum, of an astronomical observatory, and the establishing of a library. Yet not until 1844 did the national legislature really grapple with the subject.

In December of that year Senator Benjamin Tappen, of Ohio, introduced a bill which called for the founding of a library of works of science and art, in addition to a host of other objects. On January 8, Rufus Choate, of Massachusetts, rose to offer an amendment and, in an admirable speech, advocated the annual expenditure of not less than $20,000 for the gradual formation of a national reference and research library.

There was much to be said for Choate's proposal. Save for Harvard, hardly a library in the country then contained fifty thousand volumes, although one or two were approaching that number. Few had funds sufficient for increasing their holdings by systematic and considerable purchases (even at Harvard the book funds were admittedly inadequate), and they jogged along amid varying degrees of mild prosperity and dismal poverty. Almost all depended upon the chance liberality of donors to fill their shelves. John Quincy Adams's observation, that Gibbon's *Decline and Fall of the Roman Empire* could not have been written in the United States, for want of books, was not an exaggeration. Professor Jewett himself lamented that no American library could meet the full needs of students and researchers in any subject.

George Bancroft, William Hickling Prescott, and other votaries of Clio, as well as scholars like Charles Deane and George Ticknor, had to supplement the library resources at their command by assembling large private libraries at great expense for the prosecution of their labors. It was a telling comment that the *American Archives*, being edited by Peter Force and published by the federal government, was being compiled largely from the library of twenty-five thousand volumes which the indefatigable Force had collected for himself. One could not turn to the Library of Congress, which, receiving a mere $5,000 a year, was expected to furnish Congress and the government with materials, not the general public. At the very time that the country was experiencing a great interest in German literature, the Congressional library held perhaps fifty, certainly not more than a hundred, volumes in that language.

The serious student turned a longing eye toward Europe and the well-selected and invaluable library at the University of Göttingen (about 200,000 volumes); the royal libraries at Vienna (300,000 volumes), at St. Petersburg (400,000), at Munich (500,000 to 600,000) and at Paris (700,000). The Bodleian Library at Oxford, the Vatican Library, and the Royal Library at Copenhagen were in no measure duplicated in America. By 1846 the striking inadequacies of American libraries had more than once been the subject of public, not to mention private, regret, and the *North American Review* had called for remedial treatment.

It is little surprising, therefore, that Choate was joined in his proposal, known as the library plan, by a large number of the leading men of the Senate. On January 23 the Tappen bill, amended to provide that the larger part ($20,000) of the annual income of the Smithsonian fund be directed to the establishment of a general library, passed the Senate. It was lost in the shuffle of unfinished business in the House.

During the following session, Congressman Robert Dale Owen, of Indiana, introduced a bill providing that only a part of the income ($10,000) go to the library and that it be a special one. Owen asserted that Smithson's tastes were scientific and not antiquarian, and that had he desired to found a great general library he would have specifically stated that fact. In the debates that followed George P. Marsh, of Vermont, championed the library plan, going so far as to argue that the entire income be devoted to its promotion. In the end a substitute bill, which specified that no more than $25,000 be annually appropriated for the gradual formation of a library "composed of valuable works pertaining to all departments of human knowledge," passed the House and the Senate. On August 10 President Polk affixed his signature to it.

The law establishing the Smithsonian Institution provided for its organization and officers, including a board of fifteen regents and a secretary; for the construction of a building capable of housing a geological and mineralogical cabinet, a chemical laboratory, a library, a gallery of art, and lecture rooms; for the formation of a library, and for the sending to that library of a copy of all books, engravings, maps and other items entered for copyright.

The division of opinion in Congress concerning the proper administration of Smithson's gift carried over into

the Board of Regents. One of the first tasks before them—
choosing a man for the position of secretary — provoked
argument. For this post a man "distinguished as an in-
vestigator and who, besides, possessed good judgment,
catholic sympathies, and weight of character," was desired. Choate thought the secretary should be a librarian
and endeavored to effect the nomination of Jewett. But
a majority of the members of the board sought a man of
distinct scientific bent. All finally united in nominating
Joseph Henry, professor of natural philosophy in the
College of New Jersey, at Princeton.

Henry, a man of commanding presence, was then perhaps the most eminent scientist of the country. He was
forty-eight years of age, a dignified and vigorous man,
slightly above medium height, with a finely proportioned
figure made imposing by a head and features of "massive
mold." His experiments and investigations pertaining to
the properties of electric currents, solar radiation, and
the heat of sunspots had made him famous in scientific
circles the world over although, to the American people,
he was better known as the man whose discoveries had
made possible the electromagnetic telegraph. As a teacher and as a man he enjoyed the esteem of all with whom
he had contact. Although he received the offer of the
regents with gratification, Henry was reluctant to leave
academic life. Nevertheless, after much reflection, he
accepted the nomination as "a call to duty."

On December 4, immediately after Henry's election as
secretary, the regents adopted a resolution stating "That
it be recommended to the Secretary of the Smithsonian
Institution forthwith to employ, subject to the approval

of the Board of Regents, an assistant secretary, well qualified to discharge the duties of librarian." They also voted that $20,000 be appropriated to the library "for the present." Seemingly at the suggestion of Choate and others interested in the library plan, Jewett descended upon Washington armed with a letter of introduction to Henry. The Secretary received him kindly, and made known a plan he advocated for the library and his opinion on a possible division of the Institution's income. The Board of Regents had not yet agreed upon the extent or character of the library. Henry believed that the Institution should not engage in competition with other agencies of the country, and apparently said that what was needed was a working collection of scientific literature for the use of the staff and of valuable books not found elsewhere in the land. He may also have told Jewett that the $25,000 limit in the 1846 law was a maximum limit and reminded him that the regents had the power to appropriate any amount below that sum, the law merely providing that they should not exceed it. Jewett said, however, that he preferred to be instrumental in laying the foundation of a *national* library. Upon his return to Providence he abandoned all thought of being connected with the Institution.

It became very evident at this time that two parties existed among the regents, one favoring the library plan, the other desirous of advancing the cause of science. On January 25, 1847, a special committee reported a program of organization, sketched by Henry and revised and elaborated chiefly by Professor Alexander Dallas Bache. It proposed that the librarian procure catalogs of the principal public libraries of America and Europe, from which could be seen what books were valuable and were not in the United States, and what might be purchased by the Smithsonian to make its library supplemental to others in the country. To these were to be added standard reference tools, scientific publications acquired through exchange, and such works on bibliography as would make the Institution a bibliographical center to which scholars and serious students could apply, by letter or otherwise, for information as to what books existed on a particular subject and in what libraries these might be found. Since the building site for the Institution had not yet been determined, it was inexpedient to buy books until a year before the structure should be ready to receive them. But bibliographies and catalogs should be acquired.

The following day the opposing factions among the regents agreed upon a *modus vivendi* whereby one-half of the annual income was to be spent on collections in literature, science, and art, and the other half on scientific publications and researches, beginning as soon as a building had been completed—an estimated two years away. Since the museum and gallery would require only small sums for their care, it was expected that the greater part of one-half of the income would be applied to the library. That day two other resolutions were adopted:

That the secretary be requested now to nominate to the Board an assistant, who shall be the librarian, and whose salary shall commence whenever the building shall be ready for the reception of the library.

That for any service rendered by him from this time, in collecting books, making catalogues &c., he shall receive such compensation as the Executive Committee may deem reasonable.

As Jewett proved to be the preference of a majority of the board, Henry nominated him for the position of assistant secretary, acting as libarian. George M. Dallas, chancellor of the Institution, asked Henry afterward if he had done right in thus nominating Jewett, calling Henry's attention to a section of the 1846 law which stated that the secretary was to discharge the duties of librarian and keeper of the museum, although he might employ assistants to himself. The impression given by his action, said Dallas, would be that Jewett was to be the head of an independent department and an assistant to the board rather than to Henry. This was a prophetic utterance.

When notified of the board's decision, Jewett could not make up his mind whether to accept their tender of office. He was most happily situated at Brown University and he enjoyed teaching. Furthermore, he had hoped that the decision of the regents would have been to devote the major portion of the entire income to the formation of a grand, national library. Skeptical about the compromise resolutions, he was on the verge of declining the appointment when "gentlemen interested in the library plan" hastened to induce him to accept. The entire income of the fund was then $30,000. In 1846 the regents had allowed $20,000 for the library. Did he not see that if they continued to appropriate such sums annually, until the building had been finished and the compromise resolutions went into effect, he would have sufficient funds available for laying the foundation of the desired library? Could anyone be certain that the building would be completed in two years? It might be four or five. All that while, fast accumulating book purchases, copyright items, and publications received on exchange would further insure the future of a national library at the Smithsonian. On February 11 Jewett acceded to their wishes. Now that he would be inside the Institution, he could stoke the fires that Choate and Marsh had lit in Congress by keeping the eventual fulfillment of the plan before the public in his annual reports.

The library plan partisans remained vigilant, however, and, ere long, engaged in a sharp skirmish in the Board of Regents to protect their cherished design.

Congress had established Smithson's bequest as a fund, the annual interest of which was to be used to maintain and support the Institution. In 1846 it totaled $30,000, as noted above. In addition, a large sum of interest had accrued to the original gift from the time of its receipt until the passage of the 1846 law. This latter amount Congress authorized the regents to spend on the erection of a building. In 1847, having estimated the construction period as two years, the regents decided, on the recommendation of the executive committee, to erect the building gradually—taking five years—and, instead of using all of the accrued interest, to use only part of it, appropriating more than one-half of the regular annual income of $30,000 for the defrayal of building expenses, thus limiting the operating expenditures of the Institution to about $15,000 a year. The accrued interest money, from which $15,000 would be saved, was to be regarded as a new fund whose interest would be used to erect and equip the building, and whose principal would, after 1852, be joined to the regular Smithsonian fund. By 1853, therefore, there would be a greatly increased Smithsonian fund which would yield a larger interest to be applied to the active operations of the Institution.

Jewett had been informed at the time of his nomination that he would not be called into full service until the completion of the building, or for about two years. Under this new plan he could not expect to enter until March, 1852. He now earnestly entreated to be brought in before the building's completion. Choate and others, seeing a possible defeat of their library aims, rose quickly to the occasion. After warm debate, the regents voted to have Jewett commence his full service in March, 1849. Meanwhile, he was to formulate plans for initiating the acquisition of materials for the library.

In the late fall of 1847 he sent his ideas on the subject to Henry, who, on December 21, presented them to the regents. Jewett proposed that efforts be made to obtain printed and manuscript catalogs of the principal libraries of the country—the manuscript catalogs being continuations of those that had been printed—and that agreements be concluded whereby these libraries would forward their monthly or annual lists of accessions to Washington regularly. The titles cut from these catalogs and lists could be arranged in one alphabet, and their location noted, in order to form a union catalog. In addition, he suggested personal visits to libraries to become familiar with their operations and techniques, and, with an eye to cooperation, the formation of "alliances" with their librarians as indispensable in making the Smithsonian library a supplementary one for the nation as well as a bibliographical reference center.

He recommended that three classes of books be acquired: first, those immediately needed in the scientific department; second, bibliographical works, descriptions, histories, and catalogs of institutions similar in purpose to the Smithsonian; and, third, a general collection of memoirs, transactions, and journals of the learned societies of Europe and America. "These three classes of books," he noted, "will form a library quite unique, and one of great utility." He also advised that an extended list of books for future purchase be compiled, that copies of some of the most celebrated works of art and models of antiquities be procured, and that immediate steps be taken to see that the Institution should receive the books to which it was entitled under the copyright section of the 1846 law.

Shortly after, the regents resolved that he be granted not more than $1,000 from December 1847 to March 1849, for a partial carrying out of the program he had so ably outlined to them. Jewett immediately endeavored to take up some of his tasks, although his duties at Brown confined him so closely that it was difficult for him to leave Providence even for one day during the semester. He did, however, journey to Washington to offer his advice on the building plans for the library rooms, and to New York for work which Henry had assigned him, for which services the executive committee on February 8, 1848, voted him an extra $250. But soon he had to choose between dissipating his energies or failing to do justice to

29

all his responsibilities. "Finding it utterly impossible to do anything for the Smithsonian so long as" he retained his offices at Brown, he made known his decision to resign.[1] In March, 1848, he withdrew from the University.

In 1847 he had confided his plans for marriage to his close friend, Charles Folsom, librarian of the Boston Athenaeum. On April 5, 1848, Jewett wed Rebecca Green Haskins, born September 20, 1823, in Brookline, Massachusetts, the only daughter of Ralph and Rebecca Haskins. The couple made their home at Mr. Haskins' residence in Roxbury.

On April 26, Jewett, who had set about his work with his usual energy, wrote to Henry of his activities:

. . . I expect to spend the present year in Boston & hope to make good progress in the work assigned me. I have begun to collect catalogues & shall commence soon the arranging & harmonizing of them for reference. This will be a long & severe task. I will first however send you a list of bibliographical works, which will be immediately needed. I have already purchased a few books which I needed, & paid for them myself. They amount to about 13 dollars. There are about 30 dollars worth more of similar books which I need for constant reference & which I can obtain partly from Mr. [Henry] Stevens & partly from Brown University. I will send you a list of them as soon as I can ascertain the prices. I shall also need a little money some 25 or 30 dollars probably for the cards upon which to mount the titles in arranging the various catalogues in one alphabet. It is not always convenient for me to advance the money for these purposes & yet it is generally desirable & sometimes necessary to pay for them in

[1]To Joseph Henry, April 26, 1848, Archives Collection, Brown University Library.

cash. Could not the Executive Committee appropriate say 100 dolls. for such bibliographical works as I may need immediately, & for stationery & incidental expenses in my department & forward the sum to me? If there is any objection to this course I would not of course urge it. . . .[2]

He continued his purchasing and cataloging, visited several of the principal libraries of the East, and superintended the binding in New York of the first volume of the "Smithsonian Contributions to Knowledge." That fall, as the time drew near for moving to Washington, Jewett had to exercise caution in making plans, for Rebecca was expecting a child. In November he informed Henry:

. . . I have been talking over plans with my wife & she thinks that she can get ready to go with me to Washington the first week in December. The physician says that if she does not go before the middle of Dec. she ought not to go before May or at earliest April. . . .[3]

In December the Jewetts left Boston, and the following month Charles Coffin Jewett entered upon full service at the Smithsonian Institution in Washington.[4]

[2]*Ibid.*
[3]To Joseph Henry, November 17, 1848, Archives Collection, Brown University Library.
[4]Although he was not to have begun until March, the regents passed a resolution calling for his full time service and granting him full salary as of January 1, 1849.

III

Initial Projects and Problems

BEFORE COMING to Washington, Jewett had mapped out several ambitious and comprehensive projects that looked to the formation of a library whose basic collection would be one of scientific works necessary for research and reference, and such catalogs and bibliographical apparatus as would aid in locating materials in libraries throughout the country and the world, and would promote the increase and diffusion of knowledge among men. He believed that the inquiries of scholars, scientists, and research workers could be expeditiously attended to if the Institution had a catalog of the holdings of all the libraries of the United States. Henry concurred in this view and encouraged him to proceed as he saw fit. Jewett at once set out to procure three copies of each of the catalogs of American libraries. As they arrived he laid one copy aside to be preserved in its original form. From the others he clipped the titles, pasted each on a six-by-four-inch card (large enough for entering any necessary notations), and on the card stamped the initials of the library in which the title was located. To form the desired catalog, he thought he would have only to file these cards in one alphabet, and so he arranged them in drawers. Before he left Boston for Washington a sizable collection of titles had been assembled.

While work proceeded upon the union catalog, Jewett embarked upon another project suggested by the activity necessary to obtain the catalogs from libraries. "In accordance with the plan of rendering the Smithsonian Institution a centre of bibliographical knowledge," he undertook to survey the library resources of the country. In 1848 he began to send out to "public libraries" circular letters containing numerous queries as to their collections and circulation. During that year and the following he received answers to nine hundred circulars. In some instances the information supplied was so meager that he was forced either to open a personal correspondence with the librarians, which brought him several hundred letters, or to visit the libraries himself. By the middle of the year 1849 he had accumulated sufficient material for a volume and by the first of the new year his report reached Henry's desk. Formally published the next year, it bore the title, *Notices of Public Libraries in the United States of America.*

In this invaluable and pioneer work, Jewett employed the term "public libraries" to describe "libraries which are accessible—either without restriction, or upon conditions with which all can easily comply—to every person who wishes to use them for their appropriate purposes." Thus included in the survey were state, social, college, student, professional-school, incorporated-academy, learned-society, and public-school libraries. He did not list or present information on two types of libraries: Sunday-school libraries, because he could obtain no reliable statistics; and private libraries, because the federal census included these among the institutions to be enumerated, when numbering one thousand volumes and up.

In Jewett's volume each "notice" was not merely a statement of the number of volumes and such articles as loose engravings, maps and charts, pamphlets, unbound sheets of music, coins, medals, pictures, and busts in the library. It included a historical sketch of the library, a "general account of the kinds of works of which it was composed," a detailed account of its rare and valuable books and manuscripts, and computations of the rate of increase and the use made of its collections. It reported the existence of more than ten thousand libraries, containing together something less than four million volumes, and revealed, interestingly enough, that in the middle of 1849 there were only five libraries in the country possessing fifty thousand volumes or more. Harvard University, which had 84,200, led the Boston Athenaeum and the Library of Congress (50,000 each), Yale College Library (50,481), and the Library Company of Philadelphia including the Loganian Library (60,000).

Jewett's *Notices* was not, to be sure, the first survey of library resources of the land. As early as 1724 the Bishop of London had inquired of all the parish churches in Maryland regarding their facilities, including libraries. Between 1799 and 1818 Benjamin Trumbull, in the process of collecting materials for his *Complete History of Connecticut,* had written letters to leading individuals of towns in that state, asking ten questions, among them, what libraries the town had, when had they been established, and how many volumes did they contain. In 1840 Horace Mann, while secretary to the Massachusetts

Board of Education, had issued a summary of the library resources of the towns in his native state. During 1845 and 1846 Hermann Ludewig, a Dresden jurist, had published accounts of American libraries in successive issues of a *Serapeum* at Leipzig; and in 1849 Henry Barnard had brought out a list of the "public libraries" of Rhode Island. These efforts—surveys of limited areas or surveys based it appears upon secondary materials—were hardly comparable to Jewett's in the type of material used and in the details furnished. His compendium, so extensive in coverage, replete with information culled chiefly from primary sources, and admirably arranged, soon established itself as the one volume which writers on American libraries could least afford to do without. Many sought to avail themselves of its information and a few leaned heavily upon it, as Edward Edwards did while penning the sections on America in his classic *Memoirs of Libraries, Including a Handbook of Library Economy* (1859).

Jewett was well aware of the fact that several of the notices lacked completeness or thorough accuracy. He had had a difficult time in assembling the materials. Said he:

. . . No person who will consider the vast extent of the field to be surveyed, the tedious process by which most of the information is to be collected—namely, by circular letters and private correspondence—the difficulty in this busy land of getting any one to furnish minute information on such subjects, the antiquated statistics, on these matters, which survive all other changes, in gazetteers and geographies, and the fact that there is nowhere in this country a full collection of books and pamphlets relating to the local affairs of the sev-

35

eral towns and counties of the different States—no one who will consider these things, and remember that this is but *one* of the topics of inquiry to which I was required to devote my attention, and that, by the other duties of my office, I was prevented from visiting most of the libraries which I wished to describe, will be surprised if he should find that, in some instances, these accounts are not so full nor so accurate as could be desired. . . .

He requested those who received copies of the publication "to furnish corrections, additions and suggestions for a second edition, so that within a few years materials might be obtained for accurate accounts, embracing all historical facts of importance with reference to every library and every institution possessing a library." By 1853 he reported the supply of the first edition (some six hundred copies) almost exhausted, and additional material still coming in. The following year the task of preparing a new edition was turned over to William J. Rhees, whose *Manual of Public Libraries, Institutions, and Societies, in the United States, and the British Provinces of North America* appeared in 1859.

With his report on public libraries completed, Jewett was free to give more attention to the formation of the union catalog, the establishing of essential library routines and technical processes, increasing the library collection, and initiating other projects calculated to make the Institution an unrivaled bibliographical center. He continued apace on the general catalog of American libraries. During 1849 he superintended the preparation on cards of more than fifty-five thousand titles taken from printed catalogs and four thousand from manuscript catalogs. As the catalogs that came early to hand were those of several libraries in the District of Columbia and in Cambridge, Massachusetts, he soon had a small union catalog of their respective holdings. It was limited in use to individuals in Washington or to correspondents of the Institution. With Henry's approval, therefore, he branched off his general catalog scheme—he did not abandon it—that he might also make a catalog of all the books in the libraries in Washington, including "those of the several departments of the government." Perhaps he conceived the idea while examining the general catalog of the books belonging to the various libraries connected with the Navy Department of the French government, which had been published a few years previously in five large octavo volumes.

Before Jewett came to Washington the few books belonging to the Institution were in the hands of various officers, the members of the building committee, and gentlemen engaged in preparing scientific memoirs for publication. During his first year he collected, arranged, and prepared them for use. At the same time he established the procedures whereby each item was entered in an accession catalog with full and minute registration of bibliographical information, and then entered on a shelf list. By 1850, there were 6,578 items in the library collection, of which 4,233 were books.

Bearing in mind that one of the prime responsibilities of his position was to build up a collection, ("Such a depository as he [the scholar] seeks we wish to form here," Jewett had written Henry), and realizing that he faced a limited budget for purchases, Jewett set out to tap two sources that might swell its acquisitions without expense: exchanges and copyright materials.

The problem of international exchanges was then being earnestly discussed in the United States because of the efforts of Alexandre Vattemare. About the year 1824 this French ventriloquist and impersonator had become obsessed with the idea of an exchange system, among the governments and public institutions of the world, of duplicate books and art objects. Such an interchange would not have been without precedent in France, where a limited amount of exchange had been carried on with foreign countries since the latter part of the seventeenth century. Vattemare's system was founded largely on the principle that exchanges be handled by a special agent hired by the national governments; this he later extended to include those of states and municipalities. In 1840, while visiting the United States, he had presented a memorial on the subject of international exchanges to Congress, which passed a resolution favoring the idea. This had secured him the interest and cooperation of many men prominent in official life. By 1842 the cities of Boston, New York, and Baltimore had presented books to Paris, and, after December, an exchange of Continental works to America had begun through the labors of Vattemare. In 1847, on another journey to America, he had sent a second memorial to Congress and appeals to the legislatures of the states which resulted in his being appointed an agent of Congress and of a few states to see after their exchanges.

In his program of organization, submitted to the Board of Regents in 1846, Joseph Henry had suggested that part of the publications of the Institution be presented to Congress for distribution and that remaining copies be exchanged with literary and scientific institutions and sold to individuals at moderate prices. Acting upon this suggestion, as a means of diffusing knowledge and increasing the holdings of the library, Jewett compiled a list of the publications of the learned societies of the world and presented it in his annual report for 1848, together with concrete proposals on the best manner of pursuing exchanges. This report, says William D. Johnston, "became the basis for the Smithsonian exchange system" which flourished from the beginning. By the year 1853, when exchanges were being made with some three hundred foreign institutions, the Smithsonian possessed the most extensive collection of the later publications of the learned societies of the world to be found in the United States. Many of the earlier issues were wanting. In his report for that year Jewett called attention to this fact. The following year, influenced by his observations, the Institution appointed an assistant to make a catalog of all the publications of learned societies and periodicals in the library. When it was printed in 1855 and 1856, the agents of the Institution were better able to work toward filling the gaps by purchase.

The Smithsonian exchange system, which Jewett had a hand in establishing, was in no way connected with that brought about through the efforts of Vattemare. Indeed, it operated on a vastly larger scale and was based not so much on the interchange of duplicate holdings as upon the publications of the Institution itself. "While the two systems were in the process of development almost simultaneously," Elizabeth M. Richards states, "there seems to have been a parallel development with points in common, but no direct relation between the two." Jewett did not regard Vattemare's system with favor, doubtless thinking, as did many of his contemporaries, that not a few of the Frenchman's suggestions were impracticable and naïve." Not many years after his return to France, Vattemare's system began to decline in popularity. Henry Stevens, George Livermore, and others dubbed Vattemare a charlatan and his system impossible. Support was withdrawn and it collapsed.[1]

How to obtain all the materials to which the Institution was entitled under the copyright section of the organic act, and thus augment the library collection, was a perplexing problem. The law of 1846 had failed to provide for enforcement of this section. In the absence of penalties many publishers did not trouble to send the required number of copies to Washington: one to the Library of Congress, one to the Department of State, and one to the Smithsonian. Some were unaware of the directions of the statute, while still others regarded its provisions as unjust or deemed it inconvenient or unessential to comply with them. On April 26, 1848, a concerned Jewett wrote to Joseph Henry:

. . . I see by the papers that a special committee has been appointed by the House to take into consideration (if correctly reported) the *whole matter* of *copyright*. Would it

[1]After Vattemare's death, his son Hippolyte endeavored to interest the United States Department of State in resurrecting the system, but the Department, after having solicited Jewett's advice, refused its assent.

not be well to refer to this Committee the questions growing out of our 10th Section. If it be considered just & expedient to require three copies of every book, let the delivery of them be made obligatory & essential to the securing of a valid title. I have always thought that at least *two* copies should be required, because there is always danger of losing one by fire or otherwise. One of these copies should be kept in a safe depository, from which *it should never be taken,* except by order of a Court of Law. Why may not the copy for the Congress Library be relinquished? or better perhaps, the copy now required for the State Department be deposited there? We should probably be able to guard our books more vigilantly than any of the public libraries in Washington & therefore it seems to me desirable that one of the copies required should be deposited with us. I do not find among publishers any unwillingness to give two or even three copies of their publications provided they could do it without the trouble & expense of sending them to Washington. . . .[2]

But the apathy and remissness of the publishers could not be overcome by mere suggestions, and the situation grew worse. Jewett was fairly annoyed, for he wished to publish a monthly bulletin listing all the copyright works received, with full title, date of deposit and "proprietor." In his annual reports he dwelt upon the lamentable conditions that prevailed. In 1851 he noted with ill-concealed dissatisfaction that the Institution was receiving only half of the books to which it had a legal right, and in his 1853 report wrote at length upon the subject.[3] On March 3, 1855, Congress, induced in part by

[2]Archives Collection, Brown University.
[3]In 1852 he proposed, although he admitted he saw no immediate means of accomplishing the object, an international copyright exchange system.

41

his well-taken stand, passed an act authorizing the free mailing of all articles entered for copyright.

Such were Jewett's primary activities during his first years at the Smithsonian, when his efforts were directed toward two main objectives: the gathering and organization of a library collection, together with suggestions of the ways and means by which it might be supplemented and increased; and the devising of projects calculated to make the Institution a center of bibliographical information. In a position that almost daily offered challenging situations, his sense of initiative was highly stimulated, as was his naturally inventive mind. He proceeded, in response to his environment, to lay plans and fashion projects, enthusiasm gripping him at every turn. Yet it was to the realization of one particular scheme, exciting and highly original, that he unreservedly dedicated himself.

IV

The Grand Scheme: Its Origin

In 1850 Jewett, true to character, was attending to his manifold duties: administering the library, supervising the formation of the union catalog of the libraries of Washington, keeping up the labor on the general catalog of all the books in American libraries, making suggestions on exchanges and copyright materials, and devising a scheme for shelving the books in the new library wing in the western part of the building. In the midst of these activities he found himself feverishly engaged in attempting to perfect the outline of another great project.

As early as 1847, while librarian of Brown University, and possibly with an eye to using it when the time came to issue a revised edition of the 1843 *Catalogue*, he had conceived the idea of printing catalogs by means of separate stereotyped plates of individual titles. That fall he had sketched plans and communicated them to Henry Stevens, the American bibliographer, on the eve of the latter's departure for England, with a request that during his visit to London Stevens lay the plans before "gentlemen connected with the Library of the British Museum." Stevens had faithfully complied with his wishes. Still, the execution of so ambitious an undertaking depended upon its practicability, and, although Jewett had given the matter thought, he had not yet had the benefit of

43

advice on the mechanical end. It is hardly surprising, therefore, that neither response nor suggestion came to him by way of London.

While working during 1848 and 1849 upon the general catalog of American libraries, he began to consider the subject again. He had embarked upon the general catalog project expecting that, since most of the public libraries of the country then possessed printed or manuscript catalogs, all that he would have to do would be to combine the titles from their catalogs into an alphabetical arrangement on cards. The limited use to which the finished catalog might be put—already mentioned— scarcely seemed calculated greatly to facilitate research in literature and science, or to increase and diffuse knowledge among men. If only multiple copies of it could be printed and distributed to libraries throughout the land, the value of the tool would be much enhanced, Jewett thought. At this juncture he had to resolve two problems: first, whether it was wise and expedient to print the catalog at all; and second, how to print a catalog from the titles cut from library catalogs that had been compiled with so bewildering a variety of entries that it was often difficult to find one book entered in the same way in three different publications.

The question of printing library catalogs was then the subject of vigorous debate, particularly in England. In 1840 the British Museum had published the first volume of a new catalog of printed books. It filled 457 pages and contained all the titles under the letter "A" in the museum library at the end of the year 1838. From the first, Panizzi had strongly opposed printing any part of it before the entire manuscript had been completed. His view had been upheld by the several commissioners appointed by the Queen in 1847 to look into the affairs of the museum. They, indeed, had reported against printing the catalog at all and decided that only a manuscript catalog should be kept up. The chief argument against printing was that at the time the catalog was passing through the press the library was receiving new books, the titles of which could not possibly be incorporated into the body of the work. Thus, even before the catalog had been completely printed, it would be out of date. A supplement would be the only recourse, and soon that would have to be supplemented. The Library of Congress catalog furnished an excellent example of Ossa piled on Pelion. There, by 1849, the student was "obliged to grope his weary way" through a basic volume and nine supplements, and he still could not be certain that the book he sought had not been added to the collection since the last supplement had been printed.

There were only two courses open, therefore: one, to print basic and frequent supplemental volumes; the other, to maintain a manuscript catalog. Jewett believed the former preferable by far, and also that in the stereotyping scheme he had the best means of circumventing the problems involved in the printing operations. He set to work further to explore its possibilities, laboring over details and consulting with several stereotypers as to mechanical difficulties. Although their opinions were discouraging and pessimistic—they spoke of "insuperable" obstacles—he refused to accept their verdict and determined to institute experiments to satisfy himself that the plan was practical. But he was unable to do so because the Institution did not yet have its own printing office and because he found himself hemmed in by his many library duties. Regretfully, he put the mechanical matter to one side.

Jewett also saw that as long as each library followed its own cataloging rules no general catalog of the libraries of America could be constructed simply by clipping entries from pages, placing them on cards, and printing them in a volume. In order to stereotype titles he would have to have uniformity of entries. This he proposed to attain by having each library compile its catalog from a set of cataloging rules which he would devise.

As Jewett began to envision his scheme, it would embrace the publication of catalogs of individual libraries as well as a grand, general catalog of all American libraries, with the location of titles. At the center of the system, surrounded by a corps of cooperating libraries, would be the Smithsonian Institution, which would issue the rules for preparing catalogs, fashion the stereotype plates to be used in printing the catalogs of libraries that adopted the plan, and act as a depository for the plates. Each library could use these plates as often as it desired for printing catalogs or bibliographies, providing only that it reimburse the Institution for the expenses incurred in distributing the titles to their proper places, in making up pages, and in presswork.

Thus stood the general outline of the project by 1850. By that year the directors of the American Antiquarian Society and its librarian, Samuel Foster Haven, had heard of the plan. With a view to employing it in preparing a supplement to their catalog, Haven wrote to Jewett asking for details. On January 24, 1850, Jewett responded:

DEAR SIR,

I have the pleasure to acknowledge the receipt of your letter of the 17th instant enquiring my views as to the best mode of preparing a supplemental Catalogue of the Library of the Antiquarian Society. I had hoped before this time to be able to mature a plan for stereotyping by titles, in connection with a project for a general printed catalogue of all the books in all American Libraries. I have been compelled to postpone the matter, until such time as we may have a printing office of our own. Most of our funds, as you are aware, have, thus far, been absorbed by the building, & we have not been able to establish a press, or to put in operation some other important portions of our plans. I had not wished to publish the scheme which I had been thinking of for Catalogues, until I had fully matured it & had satisfied myself of its entire practicability. I am very desirous however of having the matter placed before our best librarians, that they may think upon it & offer suggestions. The plan which I propose is briefly this: To draw out in detail directions for the registrations of titles so as to secure accuracy, fullness & uniformity; to decide upon the size of type, width of page & use of capitals, italics, &c; & to arrange the minutest details of the stereotyping process. We might then propose to any librarian about to prepare a catalogue, that if the titles were thus prepared, we would stereotype them at our own expense, whether the stereotyping were done at the place where the catalogue was printed; or, whether (as might sometimes be practicable) the composition was done elsewhere & the matter sent to us for stereotyping & printing; or, finally, whether the catalogue were sent to us in manuscript to be printed & stereotyped. In this last case, we might set it up, stereotype

47

it, & print the required number of copies, the stereotyping being at our charge & the composition, press work, paper, &c, being at the charge of the Library to be immediately benefitted, or in some cases at the joint expense of that & our own institution, or sometimes perhaps entirely at our own expense. The plates would remain in our possession & might be used in printing a Catalogue of the next Library, so far as the titles were identical. Thus, after awhile, we should have a stereotyped title of every work in all the libraries which should come into the arrangement. It would be a mere matter of *im*posing anew & of press work to make of them a catalogue of all the Catalogues & to strike off a new edition of any single catalogue. The whole system might I think be made so perfect, that every Library could print at a very trifling expense, each year, a new & complete catalogue of all its treasures, &, say every two or every five years, a new general Catalogue might be issued. The cost in any case would be merely that of setting up & stereotyping the *new* titles, improving the old matter anew & of press work & paper for the requisite number of copies. One or two hundred copies would be enough for almost any library, if a new edition were each year or even every 2 or 3 years to be issued. It is easy to see that this would all work well within certain limits. The question which I wish to settle is, whether it is capable, in practice as well as in theory, of indefinite extension. The question of economy & of usefulness, require here close calculations, an exact knowledge of all the details of all the processes to be gone through with, & a consideration & careful estimation of the benefits to be derived from the scheme when once in operation. Thus far it is merely an idea. I have been at work upon the general catalogue independent of this plan of stereotyping & have made considerable progress in it. This stereotype catalogue cannot be

48

made from existing catalogues. They are most of them too inaccurate. It must be a work of years. I do not yet feel sure that it will ever be practicable. I have not yet been able to study the matter thoroughly, & therefore have not published anything on the subject. As you have however heard of the project, I am happy to be able to ask your opinion & to beg that you will favor me with any suggestions which may occur to you. . . .[1]

Jewett's exposition of the subject so impressed Haven that he immediately brought it to the attention of his friend, the Reverend Edward Everett Hale, the kindly pastor of the Church of the Unity, in Worcester. Hale, a man much interested in libraries, was fascinated by the idea and proceeded to offer several valuable and ingenious suggestions as to how the mechanical difficulties might be solved. These were soon seconded by the practical skill of "Mr. Wilcox, an electrotypist of Boston," who, after brief experimentation made an "electrotyped plate of separate movable titles," which Jewett, somewhat intoxicated with joy at the sudden turn of events, hailed as "a beautiful piece of work."

Like ripples from a pebble tossed in a pond, enthusiasm spread. While Hale and Haven energetically endeavored to solicit mechanical aid in Worcester and Boston, Jewett, fired with zeal, began to cast about for the most inexpensive material from which to construct the necessary plates. His attention was drawn to a new process of stereotyping invented by a native of Indiana, Josiah Warren. Warren, later known as America's first political anarchist and the author of several works on

[1]Correspondence Files, American Antiquarian Society.

49

political economy, suggested, as both economical and cheap, a type of clay found in his native state. Together he and Jewett set to work to fashion a plate from this material.

In the midst of these feverish activities Jewett suffered the utmost chagrin. The *Report of the Commissioners to Inquire into the Constitution and Government of the British Museum,* published in April, 1850, revealed that in February of the previous year William Desborough Cooley, in the course of giving evidence before that body, had proposed a plan for stereotyping titles similar in certain respects to Jewett's. At the time, Cooley made no mention of any other person as the originator of the scheme and, indeed, a year later offered no correction to the editor of the *London Athenaeum* when an article appearing in its pages (May 11, 1850) attributed the plan to him and bestowed much praise upon it. Jewett, when he read the report of the royal commissioners, was stung to the quick, because he had taken measures to carry his "scheme into operation several years before Mr. Cooley suggested in public a scheme in some degree similar" and because his "plans were known at the British Museum several months before Mr. Cooley brought the matter forward." With understandable vexation he took up the cudgels in defense of his priority.

Needless to say, a controversy broke out on both sides of the Atlantic that lasted for many years and acquired international character. America had Jewett, England had Cooley. France, not to be outdone, put in her bid for originating the scheme when the Chevalier de la Garde, an employe of the Bibliothèque Nationale, claimed (1850) that he had formed a very similar plan eighteen years earlier and had published a summary of it in 1845. Outdoing all the others, Charles Folsom solemnly informed the Librarians' Convention of 1853 that he had done all the claimants one better; the idea, he said, had struck him "thirty years ago." By that time, however, the storm of words was subsiding and Jewett was resting comfortably, for he and his friends, notably George Livermore and the Reverend Mr. Hale, had carefully supplied the world with all the factual information needed to remove doubts about his being the originator of the stereotyping scheme. He had been discreet in withholding his private conclusions from public consideration. Although he averred in public that his chief concern in the matter was that his scheme should not be unfavorably judged because of any impracticability in Cooley's, he had been extremely shaken when the question of priority had first been agitated. But as the years passed he faced the claims of each new challenger with philosophic calm. Doubtless he derived no little satisfaction, and had what he considered a fit revenge for his humiliation, in deluging the editors of the *London Athenaeum* with documents and pieces of evidence supporting his own claim. As he wrote to George Livermore:

. . . Now "we shall see what we shall see." I do not forget . . . what an editor once said to me. "It is very hard for us to eat our own words." . . .[2]

---

[2]January 9, 1853, Miscellaneous Manuscript Papers, New York Public Library.

V

The Grand Scheme Launched

DURING JUNE, 1850, while he and Warren wrestled with
the "clay problem," Jewett took time to write out his
catalog plan in detail. It was presented for endorsement
to the regents on July 5. They referred the matter to
Henry and the executive committee. Deeming themselves hardly competent either to criticize or properly
to evaluate it, they in turn decided to submit it to the
judgment of a commission of "literary men."

On August 16 Henry addressed identical letters to
Edward Everett, Charles Folsom, Joseph Green Cogswell, George Livermore, Samuel Foster Haven, and Edward Everett Hale. Declaring that the Institution had
"resolved to form a general catalogue of the various
libraries in the United States," he offered Jewett's scheme
as a means of accomplishing this object. It embraced
two measures: one, a plan for stereotyping the catalogs
of libraries by using separate movable title plates, drawn
up in a uniform manner; two, a set of rules designed to
ensure such uniformity and recommended for adoption
by libraries in the preparation of their catalogs. The
commission was to report upon "the practicability of
the plan presented," and "the propriety of adopting the
rules proposed."

Within a week, on August 22, Jewett revealed his plan

publicly for the first time when, at the fourth annual meeting of the American Association for the Advancement of Science, at New Haven, he read a paper, "A Plan for Stereotyping Catalogues by Separate Titles: And for Forming a General Stereotyped Catalogue of Public Libraries in the United States." He exhibited specimens of stereotyped plates of separate titles made up into pages, in common type metal, in electrotype, and in Josiah Warren's newly invented composition.

That fall the commissioners took up their task with enthusiasm and interest. Little wonder, too, for Folsom, Cogswell, and Haven were librarians, and Everett, Livermore, and Hale were men greatly interested in the development of libraries. Moreover, they were either acquaintances or, like Folsom and Livermore, intimate friends of Jewett. During the months of September and October they pored over the plan which Jewett first presented in person, and several times called him before them for interviews. After careful consideration, they were satisfied that no mechanical difficulty could be encountered which would hinder the execution of the stereotyping scheme, and likewise that the rules proposed were "drawn up with judgment and care." In their report, dated October 26, 1850, they recommended, inasmuch as the Institution did not then contain a sufficiently large library on which to experiment, that the regents obtain the requisite authority to prepare a catalog of the Library of Congress on the stereotype plan.

As Jewett's project received the commendation of the commissioners, so it won the hearty approval of Henry. The Secretary, however, desired that the Institution's library be first to have a catalog fashioned on the plan, which might then be distributed as a model. Still, he agreed to bring the suggestion of the commissioners relative to the Library of Congress to the attention of the regents for several reasons, among them that the Library of Congress "could bear the cost of the first collection of stereotyped titles better than any other library."

Before Henry could recommend any course to the regents he had to be satisfied, and Jewett had to satisfy himself, that there would be no mechanical difficulties. To solve such problems, Jewett instituted a series of experiments with Warren, seeking to blend clay and shellac to form printing blocks of unquestioned practicability. There were endless snags because there was no type foundry at hand and no real stereotyping office at the Institution. Mechanical troubles developed, and before long the assistant Jewett had trained for the work fell ill. The librarian called a halt in April, 1851. By October suitable apparatus had been readied, adequate amounts of type and materials acquired, and a stereotyping room established in the basement of the west wing of the Institution. Two months later the office was sufficiently in working order to allow the preparation of plates and the printing of a few sheets from them. Although the latter proved somewhat unsatisfactory, Jewett (paraphrasing an old saying as "Practice will give greater perfection") appended them to his annual report for the year 1851. To convince the regents and the public that his scheme was entirely practical, he continued the experiments.

Meanwhile, he refined his cataloging rules. In framing them he had turned to the ninety-one rules of Panizzi that had long been employed at the British Museum, and had simplified and improved these in the light of his observations of European and American practices and his own experience. His code embodied detailed instructions on the transcription of titles, the treatment of foreign names in alphabetizing, the choosing of subject headings, the "character of cross references," and the arrangement of bibliographical data. By way of illustration he had added examples. He had been careful to solicit the opinions of colleagues, especially Folsom, who were well versed in cataloging and its problems. Jewett's rules, soon to be published, were to establish themselves as the best procurable in America and to become, says Henry C. Bolton, "the basis of all subsequent publications of like character." Indeed, many libraries, notably that of Bowdoin College, would compile their catalogs chiefly in accordance with them, and Joseph Sabin, one of the country's leading bibliographers, would adopt them, to a considerable extent, in his great *A Dictionary of Books Relating to America, from Its Discovery to the Present Time* which began to appear in 1867. Jewett's code would continue to hold its own until Charles Ammi Cutter brought out his elaborate *Rules for a Printed Dictionary Catalogue* (1876).

By the spring of 1852, Jewett was fretful because the machinery used for the experiments had broken down and it was necessary to have new and more delicate equipment manufactured, a situation complicated by the difficulty of securing artisans sufficiently skilled for that task. On April 24 he expressed his impatience to Folsom:

55

. . . I have been at times almost discouraged about the stereotyping on account of the difficulty of getting apparatus made
with sufficient exactness. I have lost a full year by means
of the stupidity, ignorance and dilatoriness of the miserable
mechanics at whose mercy I have been placed. We have
now to wait for some pieces of apparatus to be entirely re-
constructed, but we feel now entire confidence as to the
result. I have worked very hard & have had many anxious
days over it. But I shall forget all that if I succeed. . . .[1]

Affairs soon took a happier turn. The required equipment arrived, trained workmen were hired, and the services of an accomplished mechanic secured. Jewett made
haste to prepare a complete exposition of his plan for
public distribution. That year there appeared, *On the
Construction of Catalogues of Libraries, and of a General
Catalogue, and Their Publication by Means of Separate,
Stereotyped Titles. With Rules and Examples.* In 1853
a second edition, greatly revised, was issued.

Now, with the details of the plan revealed to all, comments and criticisms could better be gathered. The
friends of the scheme and the originator loudly pro-
claimed its many advantages. They noted that the
printed catalogs of American libraries in the possession
of the Smithsonian contained some four hundred and
fifty thousand titles and that among these would be found
"not more than one hundred and fifty thousand *different*
titles." Had these libraries, having a base of three hundred thousand titles common to all, followed Jetwett's
plan, they would have saved two-thirds of the cost of
individually printing their catalogs, for the only con-

[1]Folsom Papers, Boston Public Library.

siderable expenditure to each would have been incurred in the preparation of the titles not held in general. Once a library had adopted the Smithsonian catalog system, as Jewett called it, and its first catalog had been issued, the thorny problem of supplements would be solved, for a major portion of the titles in a new edition of the catalog would be available in the plates previously used. It would merely be necessary to insert plates for works acquired by the library since the previous printing. In this manner the cost of republishing a catalog—the preparation, composition and correction of titles—would be negligible for all but the new titles.

They pointed out, too, that, because of their interchangeability, the plates might be used in the construction of bibliographies and catalogs under alphabetical, chronological, or classed arrangements. From the publication of the catalogs of individual libraries it would not be difficult to advance toward the printing of a general catalog of public libraries in the United States, with the location of the books. With such a tool at hand, said Jewett, students and scholars could more accurately learn the full extent of resources for investigation and research, interlibrary loans and exchanges among libraries could be facilitated and expanded, and the purchasers of books in public libraries could more readily determine the needs of the United States and thus help to free scholars from their "condition of provincial dependence in literary matters." He enumerated other advantages: the plan would greatly aid in the formation of an American bibliography or an account of all the books published in America. He suggested that monthly, annual and quinquennial catalogs of the copyright books received by the Smithsonian Institution might be made which "would furnish full and satisfactory records of American publications," providing legislation rectifying the defects of the copyright section of the 1846 law were passed. And, he stated,

. . . this project looks towards the accomplishment of that cherished dream of scholars, *a universal catalogue*. If the system should be successful, in this country, it may eventually be so in every country of Europe. When all shall have adopted and carried out the plan, each for itself, the aggregate of general catalogues, thus formed—few in number—will embrace the whole body of literature extant, and from them, it will be no impossible task to digest and publish a universal bibliography.

By 1853, therefore, he had set his full plan before the public. He had, to a fair degree, shown that it was practical, and had held out hopes for complete mechanical perfection with the continuance of experiments. Secretary Henry, who had given him unstinted support in the project, was now able to bring the scheme for stereotyping a catalog of the Library of Congress to the attention of the governing body of the Smithsonian. On February 12, 1853, the Board of Regents adopted a resolution requesting the secretary to call the attention of the library committee of Congress to the plan, to inform the committee that the Institution was ready to execute the proposed work, and to invite their cooperation in the enterprise. Two days later Jewett wrote Senator J. A. Pearce of the library committee:

DEAR SIR,

I have the honor to send you, herewith, the Resolutions of the Board of Regents, concerning the catalogue project, Professor Henry's letter to the Library Committee, and an estimate which I have made of the expense of the work.

I most earnestly desire the favorable action of the Committee. This seems to me the turning point of success or failure of the whole system. The expense of the first 20000 titles is the only thing that can prevent its success, with other libraries, although that expense is but a first outlay, to be surely repaid many times.

> I remain
> Most respectfully
> & sincerely
> Your obedient servant[2]

A month later, on March 3, Congress appropriated $3,000 for the preparation and publication of the catalog.

From March until July, when work upon the catalog began, Jewett continued to administer the library, supervise several projects he was attempting to push to completion, and attend to the perfection of details for the coming great endeavor. Even during this period, with the pressure of work becoming increasingly heavy, he found time to maintain social amenities with Washington acquaintances, among them Professor Spencer Fullerton Baird and his wife, and senators and representatives from New England, such as Edward Everett of Massachusetts, and James Meacham of Vermont. With friends like Livermore he kept up a heavy correspondence. From two sources he derived constant inspiration and happi-

[2]Library of Congress Papers, Library of Congress.

ness: his religion and his family life. A staunch believer in church attendance, he faithfully practiced his beliefs as an Episcopalian. As husband and father he showered tender affection upon Rebecca and little Rebecca Rose (born February 21, 1849). Every spring he and his wife would avidly anticipate their vacations in New England, and when, in the summer, the heat of Washington grew oppressive they would gladly escape to Quincy, Massachusetts, where they found required rest and bracing breezes by the seashore. Not every such respite was devoted to complete relaxation, for in 1850 and in 1851 Jewett went so far as to employ much of his time in attending to Smithsonian Institution work that he could not perform in Washington, a course, it should be emphasized, not urged upon him by Henry or any official of higher authority, but rather by his temperament, by his impulsive eagerness to solve problems by means of large and comprehensive programs. As the problems multiplied, after 1848, so did the number of projects. By 1853 the stereotyping scheme alone had been expanded to include, besides the Library of Congress catalog, the printing of a bibliography of works on education, a catalog of bibliographical works in the Smithsonian library, and a list of the periodical publications received by that library. Work on the first of these had started prior to January of that year and Jewett expected it to come from the press before 1854. At the same time negotiations were pending with Henry Stevens, in London, in regard to the publication by the Smithsonian of a *Bibliographia Americana* which Stevens would compile. These years saw the manifestations of what might be called Jewett's "juggler's complex," that irresistible urge to keep three, four, or five objects whirling through the air simultaneously.

To the building of red-brown sandstone with arcaded porte-cochere and flag tower that housed the Smithsonian Institution came many a visitor to Washington, several purposely to inspect the library and some to study Jewett's methods. During the year 1850, when the library contained slightly more than nine thousand articles, approximately sixteen thousand individuals flocked to inspect it. In the spring of 1853 Willard Fiske, of Cornell University, calling there, saw a collection of some twenty-five thousand articles and, in a letter to the *Syracuse Chronicle*, wrote that "several interviews with its learned and friendly Librarian, Professor Jewett, enabled me to obtain some insight into the manner of conducting the bibliograpical part of its labors."

To observers like Fiske, Jewett could point out the projects planned or in progress and the procedures devised for the handling of routine affairs, the accessions catalog and the shelflist up to date, the books cataloged on cards, the numbered library shelves, and the books upon them that had been given fixed location numbers. He could show a "Finding List," an alphabetical list of the books in the library with their shelf numbers—a tool fashioned for the use of readers.

Yet, privately, he might well have deplored the physical arrangements. From the first he had found his patience and ingenuity taxed, and himself hampered, in establishing such essential processes as cataloging and in pushing ahead with his projects, by the inadequate facilities at the Institution. The construction of the building had gone forward slowly. In January, 1849, when he had come to Washington, he had had to locate himself in the upper rooms of the east wing which had not then been completely constructed. Before the close of the year, the west wing having been finished, he moved thither only to find himself cramped in the space set aside for the reading room of the library and staff workrooms. Seeing his *Notices* through the press had proved a heavy trial, and he had complained to George Livermore about these conditions. Still, when the main edifice should be finished and the library reading room (ninety by fifty feet) which had been planned for the first story be completed, he would be able to rejoice, he hoped. In 1853, so slowly had the construction work progressed, Jewett was forced to resort to makeshifts. In the westwing quarters, where book cases had been installed for the *temporary* library, books stood in double rows on most of the shelves. The large, principal library room had a stone floor and could not be heated, and several assistants contracted colds while working there. Many books had been impaired by the attendant dampness, and not a few pamphlets and papers had to be removed to the basement. This, of course, was the side of the coin seen by few.

By July, 1853, Jewett had completed his plans for work on the Library of Congress catalog. It was to contain a full and accurate description of the books in the library, with each title being as far as possible exactly transcribed from the original, and was to contain annotations where essential, copious cross references, and an index of subjects. The end product was to conform to the principles he had once recounted to Samuel Foster Haven:

. . . A Library without a catalogue is like a body without an eye. The more perfect the catalogue, the more useful the Library. There may reasonably be various opinions as to the best mode of preparing a catalogue; but the more I have reflected upon the subject, & the more experience I have had in the use of them, & the more knowledge I have had of the experiences of others,—the more I am confirmed in the opinion that alphabetical catalogues are by far the most convenient & useful. The Index too should be alphabetical, though under some words the recognized divisions of the subjects named may appropriately be followed. The more minute the Index, the better. . . .[3]

In July operations began. There was an initial setback. The skilled assistant on whom Jewett "had so much relied" fell ill, and he himself had to supervise the three catalogers, two compositors, the stereotyper, and a boy assistant. At best progress was slow. Work upon the general catalog of all American libraries was soon suspended and all hands concentrated upon the Library of Congress catalog. The grand scheme had, however, been safely launched. In September Jewett hurried to New York to attend the Librarians' Convention.

[3]To Haven, January 24, 1850, Correspondence Files, American Antiquarian Society.

VI

Convention Interlude

THE IDEA OF A convention of "librarians and others interested in bibliography" first occurred to Charles B. Norton, a New York bookseller, agent for private and public libraries, and publisher of *Norton's Literary Gazette and Publishers' Circular*, a monthly, and *Norton's Literary and Educational Register*, an annual. Norton proposed his idea in an editorial in the *Gazette*, July 15, 1852, and he thereafter advocated it from time to time in the columns of that periodical. The following year his editorial assistants, Daniel Coit Gilman and Seth Hastings Grant, and their close associate, Reuben Aldridge Guild, seem to have conferred among themselves and appointed Grant, then the librarian of the New York Mercantile Library, as intermediary between Norton and Jewett in laying plans for a convention.

Jewett at this time was one of the more eminent librarians of the country. His various accomplishments as librarian of Brown University and the Smithsonian Institution had established his reputation beyond all doubt. Everywhere his abilities were highly praised, his truly inventive mind respected, and his ingenious projects and his energetic efforts to carry them to completion greatly admired. Seldom was a large-scale library project undertaken that did not come to his desk for criticism or ap-

64

proval, for, as George B. Utley says, "much weight was given to his opinion." For years, as a man "imbued with the spirit of co-operation," he had been convinced, not only of the need for co-operation among the libraries of the country in all types of common endeavors that lent themselves to co-operative effort, but of the need for a permanent organization of librarians whereby such effort might best be promoted. His position throughout the library world was then of such unquestioned prominence that Norton had to secure his co-operation if any convention were to be a success. It was to Jewett, therefore, that he and his editorial assistants turned for advice and aid in forming plans for a conference of librarians.

In the spring of 1853 Grant and Jewett opened a correspondence on the subject. During April Norton himself paid Jewett a visit in Washington and was pleased to find him very much in favor of the idea. Jewett agreed to put his signature to a call for a conference, providing only that Joseph Green Cogswell and Charles Folsom did likewise, for he had no desire "to appear prominent in the matter." He pledged Norton his fullest co-operation and the complete employment of whatever resources his position or name might command, although he was then in the midst of preparing a detailed schedule of operations for the congressional library catalog.

After a great deal of corresponding among leading librarians and individuals interested in libraries, a call to a convention to be held in September appeared in the *Gazette*, May 15, 1853. Norton, visiting England in July, endeavored to persuade Panizzi to attend, and Jewett, who esteemed Panizzi as the prince of librarians, joined him in the attempt.[1] Panizzi gave the matter serious consideration, but was forced to decline the extended invitation as he could obtain no help from the trustees of the British Museum toward payment of his traveling expenses. Jewett also wrote to other librarians abroad, trying to get them to attend, and made attempts to interest those at home whom he could reach personally. Almost a month before convention time he wrote Grant that he felt somewhat discouraged, because:

. . . Since the call was published, I have seen but very few who would be likely to take an interest in the convention. I have found some, on whom I had counted, who seem unwilling to take any active part. The fact is our fraternity are generally very quiet, unostentatious men, not accustomed to public speaking, or fond of exhibiting themselves. . . .[2]

This was premature despair. On the appointed day (September 15), in the chapel of New York University, Jewett was one of eighty-two men who had journeyed from thirteen states in order to represent forty-seven libraries.

Numbered among the assembled were the most distinguished or most promising librarians of the day. Daniel

[1] There was strong opposition to Panizzi in Parliament and among literary men like Thomas Carlyle, not because he was incompetent, but because, as William F. Poole says, "he was a foreigner and presumed to instruct Englishmen." When in 1847 he came to "trial" before the Commissioners to Inquire into the Constitution and Government of the British Museum, Jewett wrote a warm letter praising Panizzi's accomplishments to Henry Stevens, a communication which the investigating body heard with considerable respect.
[2] To Seth Hastings Grant, August 16, 1853, in George B. Utley, "The Librarians' Conference of 1853" (unpublished ms.), p. 42.

Coit Gilman, destined in some twenty years to head the first school established primarily for graduate studies (Johns Hopkins University), came from the Linonian Library at Yale. Also present was William Frederick Poole, librarian of the Mercantile Library of Boston, soon to pass to the Athenaeum of that city and thence to the Middle West, where he was to lay the solid foundations of not one, but two great institutions—the Chicago Public Library and the Newberry Library. Samuel Foster Haven, the forty-seven-year-old librarian of the American Antiquarian Society in Worcester, who later embellished a distinguished library career with scientific writing in the fields of archaeology and history, attended. So did Charles Folsom, librarian of the Boston Athenaeum, who had earlier been librarian of Harvard College, (Nestor to his colleagues by reason of his fifty-nine years), Reuben Aldridge Guild, Jewett's successor as librarian at Brown University, and Lloyd P. Smith, head of the Philadelphia Library Company. Others, like John William Wallace, librarian of the Law Association of Philadelphia, the Reverend Samuel Osgood, a Unitarian minister of New York who represented the Athenaeum of Providence, and Edward Everett Hale, fated to be chiefly remembered by posterity as the author of *The Man Without a Country*, but now representing the Young Men's Library Association, also took part in the proceedings.

Among the gentlemen of note unable to be present were George Livermore and Joseph Green Cogswell.

Jewett, though but thirty-seven years of age, was the most prominent man at the convention. Hardly had the initial meeting been called to order by Folsom when, on a motion of Guild, Jewett was unanimously elected president. Upon taking his chair he thus addressed those gathered:

It must be highly gratifying to those who signed the call for this Convention to notice the response which it, this morning, receives. To every one who knows the nature of a librarian's duties,—the details which consume his days, and render absence from his post impossible, except at the cost of severe labor on his return,—it must be manifest that we have met at considerable personal sacrifice. We obey some strong and wide-felt impulse in incurring the expense and the trouble of this gathering.

We have no peculiar views to present, no particular set of measures to propose. We meet without preparation. No order of business has been arranged. Our proceedings must be spontaneous as our meeting. It is not important that they be systematic and formal. We come to receive and act upon suggestions. We are not here for stately debate, for conspicuous action, much less for an exhibition of ourselves. These things are foreign from our vocation, and not congenial with our tastes. We meet for familiar, informal, conversational conference, where each may take his part, and no one be prevented from contributing his share to the profits of the enterprise, by his inexperience in public speaking, or his inability to make elaborate preparation. Those gentlemen connected with the public press who honor us with their presence, must have been attracted hither by a scholarlike sympathy with our quiet pursuits, which lead them to appreciate our feelings in this respect, in the reports which they may give.

In our assembling to-day we obey the impulses of our peculiar civilization. We are pre-eminently a reading people. In Prussia the whole population are taught to read; but a distinguished citizen of that country, who had traveled in the United States, once expressed to me the difference between his own countrymen and the Americans, by saying: "Our people *can* read, your people *do* read." The generally diffused love of reading, for the sake of gaining information, has led to the establishment of a large number of libraries, so that, in the number and general diffusion of small collections of books, we are richer already than any other country in the world. Reading creates the desire to read more, and select reading increases the desire to read profitably. Hence, in every village the questions are asked: "How shall we get good books? How shall we keep them? How shall we use them?" To consult on the best replies to questions like these, is one of the objects of our assembling to-day.

Another demand of our peculiar civilization is, for the means of thorough and independent investigation. We wish to own no men as masters. We intend to re-examine all history from our own American standpoint, and we must re-write it, where we find its facts have been tortured to teach the doctrines of injustice and oppression. The mental activity of this country is surveying every field of research, literary, scientific, aesthetic, industrial, and philanthropic. It requires to know what others have done and thought, that it may itself press farther outward. This country, therefore, demands the means of the amplest research, and this demand must and will be met.

These views have impressed themselves deeply upon our minds, as we are the appointed custodians of the literary treasures of the country, and have led us to desire mutual assistance and concentration of efforts in providing for these intellectual necessities of our American life. For our present meeting it has been proposed to adopt the simplest form of organization; to appoint, besides a president and a secretary, a business committee to receive suggestions and propositions, and arrange the order of proceedings for each day's session. I unite most cordially in the hope which I have heard expressed this morning, that this Convention may be the precursor of a permanent and highly useful association.

When Jewett, in this address, said that the members of the convention met "without preparation," he employed the phrase in a very general sense indeed. He could scarcely have otherwise seriously included himself, for he came to the convention fully expecting to speak at length, not only on the Smithsonian Institution, but upon the stereotyping project. In August he had written Grant that he desired to bring the latter forward for full discussion. And this he did.

On the second day of the convention, after having earlier presented its members with copies of an unfinished work entitled the *Smithsonian Catalogue System*, Jewett took the floor and "held it for nearly the entire morning." He discoursed first on the Smithsonian Institution and its library. Of its coming role as a great national library of reference and research he was firmly convinced and stated that he had always believed that such a goal would be realized and that it was "sure to be accomplished," if not by the expenditure of Smithsonian funds, by other means such as Congressional appropriations and "donations and bequests from the rich." He then proceeded to give an elaborate account of the stereotyping scheme. This topic had aroused so much interest and speculation that he felt the gentlemen assembled might wish to hear of it in detail from its originator. The scheme, indeed, was the most exciting subject on the agenda, and the newspapers devoted more space to it than to any other topic, several, says George B. Utley, "printing Jewett's speech in full."

In the course of his presentation Jewett took occasion to meet a criticism to the effect that the plates, after having been used often, would become worn, and that when new plates were inserted for reprinting a catalog, they would appear different to the eye on the finished page. The number of copies printed would be so small, he explained, that it would be years before any appreciable difference between the old and new plates would be discernible; even runs of one hundred thousand copies would result in little observable difference. He further stated that the material being used was harder than ordinary type metal and would resist the wear of the press longer. Although he did not participate in the discussion, William F. Poole, while appreciative of the boldness of the stereotyping plan, thought that the plates fashioned by Warren would prove mechanically impossible. Well mixed were humor and prophecy when he acidly labeled the scheme "Professor Jewett's mud catalogue." But the convention on the whole was swept up on a wave of enthusiasm and placed on record both its approval of the idea of a great national library to be supported by the federal treasury and administered by the Smithsonian Institution, and its endorsement of the stereotyping scheme.

Though they may have met "without preparation" or a predetermined order of business, the other members of the convention were not lost for words or ideas. There were speeches on "popular libraries" and "public libra-

71

ries," with Osgood and Hale leading the discussions and insisting that these libraries be established in every town. The two ministers were thinking of institutions to be supported by the subscriptions of their members, and not of public libraries in the modern sense of the term. The idea of public libraries supported by municipal or town expenditures was "just beginning to get a hold on the interests of" America and Great Britain. To be sure, there were examples at Peterborough, New Hampshire, at New Bedford, Massachusetts, and at Manchester and Liverpool, England, of free, tax-supported libraries. In the main, however, the great day of the public library had not yet dawned.

There were suggestions, too, for possible projects, among them one for an "index of American news and chronology of important events for the last 125 years," and another for a catalog of standard works relating to America. Committees were appointed to memorialize Congress to provide for a more satisfactory distribution of public documents, and to take steps to secure the transmission of complete sets of the statutes-at-large of each state to the Smithsonian Institution, which would then distribute them to every incorporated or public law library of the United States. Before the convention drew to a close, four outstanding resolutions had been adopted: one favoring the establishment of "public libraries" in every town; another approving the plan and execution of Poole's *Index*, the second edition of which had been on exhibit for three days; a third proposing the compilation of a library manual, to concern itself with plans for library edifices, with the most approved method of preparing and printing catalogs, with the best administrative and organizational principles and practices of a library—officers, laws, regulations, funds—and with a list of works best suited to libraries of various sizes, from five hundred to one thousand volumes. This manual was to be prepared "through the agency of the Smithsonian Institution" and, of course, would be in Jewett's hands. A fourth resolution called for the appointment of a committee, of which Jewett was made a member, to draft plans for the formation of a permanent librarians' association, and to call a meeting in Washington, presumably upon his advice as to the opportune time.

VII

Compromise Falls to the Ground

As JEWETT, who had been "looked up to and lionized" at the Librarians' Convention, retraced his steps to Washington, he was undoubtedly troubled and disturbed, and with reason. He was returning to a position that was becoming daily more insecure, a climate of work he felt to be hostile, and an institution whose affairs were presided over by a man he regarded with loathing. That he had been under a great strain during the Librarians' Convention seems not to have been suspected by his colleagues in general, although he had confided his innermost feelings to his friends. His remarks there concerning the Smithsonian Institution and its library had been able and, in places, eloquent. It was with fervor that he had spoken of its future position as a great national library. He had been gratified by the passing of the various resolutions upholding that objective and his stereotyping scheme, for they and the popularity he enjoyed at the gathering had lifted up his spirits. But they were to be of little use or comfort to him once he had taken up his duties at the Institution again.

Joseph Henry had not long been secretary of the Smithsonian Institution in 1846 before he formed definite ideas on those aspects of the affairs and policies of the Institution that had so long agitated Congress. He was not in favor of the library plan. He believed, in brief, and so stated in his first annual report to the regents, that "increase of knowledge" would be furthered, not by providing lectures and a library, but by stimulating and supporting original scientific research through projects at the Institution, or through grants to outside workers. To him the phrase "diffusion of knowledge" meant primarily the publication and widest possible distribution of papers embodying the results of original research in the fields embraced by the sciences. Smithson's prime interest in life had been scientific investigation, he said. Was it not logical, therefore, that the Institution should be primarily a center of scientific research, and that most of the annual income should be directed to the realization of that essential purpose? He had only criticism for those parts of the congressional act providing for the diversion of a portion of the income to the support of a museum, an art gallery, and a library. But he felt that a conscientious performance of his duty required strict compliance with the provisions of the 1846 law. He did not fail, however, to seize upon every occasion that presented itself, to press home to the Board of Regents and Congress alike the crucial matter of the division of the income embodied in the compromise resolutions of 1847.

When Jewett accepted his position at the Institution in 1847 Henry's lack of enthusiasm for the library plan was already known to its proponents. They had been delighted with Jewett's favorable decision, so strongly was he devoted to the cause. It had been hoped that he would keep the library plan before the public in his annual reports, thus carrying forward the propaganda

75

initiated by Choate and Marsh, and that he would labor incessantly on its behalf within the Institution, standing guard lest Henry seek to sacrifice library interests to those of science. Upon entering into office Jewett complied with duty while indulging in expectations.

By March, 1853, Henry and Jewett, the two men who had begun their association with mutual respect and friendship, found themselves bitter antagonists. In slightly more than four years they had reached a level in personal relations where, to all practical purposes, civil conversation between them had ceased. Several factors had contributed to the situation: the manner of Jewett's appointment, the exorbitant construction expenses, and the compromise resolutions.

The manner of Jewett's appointment and the title he bore served to convince him that he was to be an assistant to the Board of Regents and head of an independent department, with his own funds and the right to make his own policies. He regarded himself, therefore, not as a subordinate of Henry's, but rather as a coequal. His early duties included, in addition to those pertaining especially to the library, aiding the secretary "in editing the publications of the institution and in the other duties of his office," among them, correspondence. Soon after he came to Washington, Henry discovered to his great surprise that Jewett would not render any assistance in the general business of the Institution unless it were given entirely in his own name. Finding that he could do nothing to move him from this stand, Henry left him free to take exclusive charge of the library, and when Professor Spencer Fullerton Baird entered the

76

service in 1850 to take charge of the museum, the Secretary gave him the supervision of printing and exchanges and assigned him some correspondence labors. Under his unhappy assumption of independence, Jewett from the first began to consider himself "above the mere care of books," and to demand assistants. In time he had three attending to routine library duties, and many others employed on the cataloging and stereotyping experiments.

A further cause of ill feeling stemmed from the provision that the compromise resolutions were not to go into effect "until the completion of the building." In an effort to erect it gradually and increase the principal of the Smithsonian fund, the regents, as noted hereinbefore, had decided, not without strong protests from Henry, to give a large portion of the annual income to construction work. How much went in that direction may be gathered from the fact that less than one-eighth of the entire amount expended annually from 1847 to 1854 was given to scientific research and publications. More lamentable, to Jewett's way of thinking, was the fact that, although an effort had been made in 1846 and 1847 to adhere to the spirit of the 1846 law and to devote to the library a substantial part of the annual $25,000 allowed by Congress, the amount of the appropriation had decreased each year to the point where, in 1853, the library received a mere $874. If any adequate foundation for a library was to be laid before the building was completed, if the library was to prosper and become the basis for the hoped-for national library, it must receive the maximum allowed by law, not the minimum necessary to meet its stipulations. As Jewett saw the annual sum granted the library diminish before his eyes he became increasingly disquieted. Henry, meanwhile, was aware that science, particularly publications and research, was suffering from the same cause. That all possible funds, save those directed to building purposes, must be channeled to its promotion seemed absolutely necessary. For this reason he not only voted with the executive committee of the regents year after year to pare down the money for the purchase of books for the library, but to cut its expenses to the bone, and before long felt it his duty to argue for the elimination of both the library and the museum, or at least their support from other than Smithsonian funds. With an eye to the future completion of the building, he thought it best also to move against the compromise resolutions—the keystone of the relationship between himself and Jewett. But by 1853 nothing definite had been decided upon or done.

From the first days of the Institution both Henry and Jewett had determined what its coming role should be, Henry expecting it to become a bulwark of scientific knowledge, Jewett believing it would develop into a great national library. Their differences were first revealed in their annual reports. In his report for 1850 Henry noted:

Though almost every one will admit the value of libraries, and the importance of collecting in this country as great a variety of books as possible, yet it may well be doubted whether the accumulation of a large number of books, which are to be found in almost every library of the country, is, in the present state of funds, to be expected or aimed at.

He further pointed out that the library being assembled by Jewett contained works that could in no way benefit the scientific scholar, and that, even if half of the annual interest of the fund were expended on the library, this portion of the income would be insufficient to collect and support a "miscellaneous library" of the first order. In his report for the next year Henry did not hesitate to state that the funds of the Institution should not be burdened with the expense of preserving a copy of every book originally published in the United States, and suggested that there might well be a bibliographical bureau at the Institution, without a library.

By 1853 Henry, in blunt fashion, was recapitulating his former views, and calling attention to the fact that "though a large library connected with the Institution would be valuable in itself, it [was] not essentially necessary to the active operations." To what he hoped might be the deserved fate of the library, he was now prepared to add that of the museum. His annual reports thereafter were given to strong reiterations of these opinions.

And what of Jewett's reports? Professor Jewett, though he advanced the national library idea with regularity, was a model of restraint for at least three years. By 1853, however, it was time to speak out, and speak out he did. In January, 1850, he had "begged leave" to present his report for the year 1849 to Henry; in December, 1850, he had opened his report for that year with the words ". . . it again becomes my duty to present to you my annual report upon the affairs of the Library." In 1852 one could detect a slight change in approach, for the report of activities began crisply, "in compliance with my official duty, I present to you, at this time, a report upon the affairs of the library during the year 1851." But the report presented to Henry in January, 1853, marks a complete break with the past. Certain incidents, soon to be related, had so irritated Jewett that he could not contain himself. In endeavoring to show no equivocation on the subject of the future of the library, he was moved to state his case in a tone that was firm and, in places, too defensive.

This report did not begin with an introduction, or with any statement about "compliance with duty." Rather, Henry was addressed thus:

Sir: The following table exhibits the number of books and other articles added to the library during the year 1852, with the sources from which they have been received: . . .

The report went on to state briefly the affairs of the library and to expatiate upon the points in dispute between Henry and Jewett. Jewett made out an elaborate case for the acquisition, under the copyright provisions of the 1846 law, of all types of materials. These materials were of course to be the basis of the anticipated national library:

It should be particularly observed that any article, however apparently worthless, acquires value and importance as an integral part of a complete collection. A collection of all the productions of the American press would, if perfect and entire, teach lessons which could not be gleaned from its parts.

It would show the extent of the literary labors of the time.

It would show the proportionate attention to the various departments of learning.

It would show, from year to year, the increase or decrease of interest in particular pursuits.

It would show the comparative literary fertility and wealth of different portions of the country.

It would show the progressive improvements in the subsidiary arts of paper-making, binding, engraving, and so forth.

He boldly stated that he was concerned about supplying the wants, not only of "all literary investigators," but, indeed, the wants of the historian, the philosopher, the artist, and the statesman. Further along came the core of the matter:

There ought, therefore, to be in every country one complete collection of everything published—one library, where everything printed should be garnered up, treated as of some importance; for, although in the multitude of libraries everything may be preserved somewhere, yet, from being scattered about, and from there being no one place where the student would be *sure* of finding all that he might seek, many books would be practically lost.

This statement derived from the premise that "a large library of reference is likely to be formed" in Washington and that the Institution should, "without prejudice to other interests," do all possible to aid in forming a "complete treasury of the materials for literary pursuits which is the *beau-ideal* of the bibliographer." Jewett was content that the congressional library should become a purely legislative one.

The issue had been joined, and the public given its first view of the opponents leveling their lances. So far did their relations deteriorate that, when the printed report for 1853 appeared, readers could detect in Jewett's portion, not firmness, but hostility, not reasoned defense, but passion. Yet these were but mild, outward manifestations of an impending crisis. Within the Institution principles and personalities were doing battle.

About the middle of December, 1852, there occurred the first of several personal scenes between Henry and Jewett. Henry, worried over the large amount of money going into the construction of the building, called Jewett to his office and expressed his desire to modify or even abandon the compromise resolutions without general public discussion. He asked Jewett to cooperate in this endeavor, and suggested that it might probably be better for him to occupy himself with the stereotyping scheme and bibliographical works instead of working toward the formation of a large library. Jewett replied that he would consider it treacherous for him, the head of the library, to consent to what he termed its overthrow. Henry answered that Choate and the "literary men" had given up the library plan. Jewett warmly denied that they had either done or intended to do so. Tempers rose. Henry, seeing that he was getting nowhere with gentleness, now took a sterner tone. He said that he would carry out his plans with respect to the compromise resolutions and warned Jewett that he would have to take the consequences for refusing to cooperate.

The assembling and preparation for the press of the report for 1852 brought about a heightening of personal animosities and an unfortunate explosion. Jewett's manuscript report for that year contained an elaborate criticism of Henry's of the year previous. Henry, after having

82

received and perused the manuscript, returned it to Jewett, pointing out that the critical parts were not proper and ought to be stricken out. Some time elapsed, and Jewett submitted the manuscript once again, with the "offensive matter" still in it. Henry now officially summoned him to his office. Jewett rushed in, in a towering rage and "in a very angry manner" demanded to know why Henry had sent for him by a servant. "He said he was a gentleman and would not be treated as a subordinate, or words to that effect." Henry, who was not to be intimidated or rushed off his feet in this manner, held his ground and compelled Jewett to omit the objectionable passages in the report. He informed him that he had consulted a lawyer and discovered that he, Henry, had the power to "turn" Jewett out. The librarian retorted that his friends expected that he would continue to champion the cause of a large library. Furthermore, he said, Henry would not dare to dismiss him, for "the attempt would shake the Institution to its center." The interview ended and, thenceforth, as the result of this clash, most of the business transactions of the two men were conducted in writing.

On March 12, 1853, Henry, in a meeting of the regents, brought up the income matter, and a special committee, consisting of James A. Pearce, James M. Mason, Richard Rush, John W. Maury, Joseph G. Totten, Alexander Dallas Bache, and James Meacham, was appointed to investigate and report on the subject of the distribution of the income "in the manner contemplated by the original plan of organization." More than a year was to pass before their report would be available.

In September, 1853, a third miserable exchange took place between Henry and Jewett. The Secretary called Jewett to his office. He entered and both men seated themselves side by side at a table. After a short silence Henry turned and looked Jewett full in the face. "I perceive that I have traitors in my camp," he said. This outburst was occasioned by the knowledge Henry had received that an intimate friend of Spencer Baird had submitted an article to *Putnam's Magazine* in which Henry was criticized, and that, seemingly, Baird had supplied the facts. Henry was human and not without fault, and on this day was probably not in a pleasant and conciliatory frame of mind. Since taking office, he, his policies, and those of the Institution authorities had come under fire from some sections of the public. To be criticized from the outside was one thing. Henry, however, could not entertain the idea that critics were receiving their ammunition from those in the employ of the Institution. Although the Secretary had Professor Baird in mind when making his remarks about "traitors," Jewett did not fail to catch the overtones. Henry went on to assert that his assistants must work in harmony with him or they must resign. Jewett, aroused, expressed great and indignant surprise at such a claim, and then inquired sarcastically whether the assistants were bound to obey or resign should Henry require them all, when they came to the Institution each morning and merely saw him, to "bow down and kiss his feet." These remarks, which Henry may well have considered personally insulting, led to worsened relations between the two men. Events shortly occurred which brought the entire matter of the struggle within the Institution to public attention.

About January, 1854, a series of attacks on the policy pursued by Henry commenced in several newspapers. The lines of argument bore such striking similarities to those advanced by Jewett that Henry assumed that the attacks, penned in a majority of instances by very close friends of Jewett, had all been instigated by him. Before long some of the articles had been reprinted in pamphlet form and were being widely distributed by both Jewett and his friends. The public was made even more aware of the controversy when John W. Maury, then mayor of Washington and, ex-officio, a regent, received a visit from an intimate friend of Jewett's who gave him to understand that he would lose his office as mayor if he did not vote the "right way" as a member of the special committee appointed by the regents. He refused to cringe before threats, and just before election time two letters against his candidacy appeared in the *Washington Star*. One of the editors of the paper informed Henry that the person who had paid for and inserted the letters was one of the men employed by the Institution in its stereotyping operations. At this juncture the individuals involved in the ever-widening spiral seem to have redoubled their efforts. Jewett, growing daily more alarmed, wrote Folsom on February 9:

. . . Prof. Henry is pushing his plans of late in such a way as to put in imminent peril the very existence of the institution. How it all will end it is impossible to see, but the whole matter is to me ineffably disgusting & I would rather dig clams for a living than stay here as of late. . . .[1]

[1]Folsom Papers, Boston Public Library.

His exasperation at Henry's course was only increased by his anxiety over the successful prosecution of the work on the Library of Congress catalog. Before the close of 1853 some six thousand volumes had been cataloged, of which four thousand were in the field of ancient history. By February, 1854, the *Catalogue of the Library of Congress. Chapter I. Ancient History. Complete to January 1854* had come from the press. Jewett sent a copy to Folsom for criticism, and begged him to write a letter approving the work, that he might show to the library committee of Congress. Additional funds were needed because in preparing and publishing this part he had used two-thirds of the appropriation. "The cataloguing was thus costing about 33½ cents a volume," William Johnston notes, "whereas the actual outlay upon the former catalogues of the Library [of Congress] had not exceeded 5 cents per volume." Still, Jewett's volume, which had been published "at the suggestion of the chairman of the Library Committee as a specimen of the proposed work," evidently impressed the Congressmen. On May 31 an additional $5,000 was granted for its continuation. But the measure brought cold comfort to Jewett; the difference of opinion between Henry and himself had reached a critical stage.

VIII

Impasse

THE SPECIAL committee appointed by the regents to examine the matter of the distribution of income, in an effort to be objective and give consideration to both sides of the question, invited the chief defender of the interests of the library to prepare and submit a written paper, setting forth his views. Jewett was nervous and excited, as indeed everyone else who was deeply involved appears to have been. Instead, however, of confining his remarks to the future distribution of the income, he seized the opportunity to express himself freely and to give vent to his mounting emotions, and coupled a vigorous assault on Henry's motives and honor with harsh criticism of the Secretary's annual reports. Henry, needless to say, had his tale to tell. In any case, the committee's report of May 20, 1854, put an end to the source of controversy.

With only one dissent, the committee placed itself on record as against the compromise resolutions and the library plan.[1] It stated emphatically that the national legislature had not intended the principal instrument of the Institution for increasing and diffusing knowledge to take the form of a public library. This was not the

[1] James Meacham later submitted a minority report, upholding the library plan *in toto*.

law; it was not the will of Smithson. The building up of a great library not being the principal object of the Institution, it was not therefore advisable to make an equal division of income for the benefit of the library. The committee took completely the view of Henry in noting:

What we want, and what the act of Congress contemplates, is not a collection of everything which learned dullness and literary folly as well as real wisdom and sound science have put into print—a vast and unwieldy repertory, in which the trash as well as the precious may be found—but a library of *valuable* books pertaining to all departments of human knowledge.

Pointing out that Congress did not specify in 1846 that a full $25,000 be annually appropriated, and that it vested in the Board of Regents the power to spend money on the library in any manner they wished and of any amount below that maximum limit, the committee made its chief recommendation, namely, that the compromise resolutions of January, 1847, "requiring an equal division of the income between the active operations and the museum and library, when the buildings are completed, be . . . repealed." It also declared, Meacham alone dissenting, that the paper it had solicited from Jewett had shown excessive hostility and insubordination.

Since the best interests of the Institution could nowise be promoted as long as the intense personal situation between Jewett and himself existed, Henry came to the painful decision that Jewett would have to be dismissed. To be certain, however, that he had specific authorization, he resolved to delay the move until at the coming meeting of the regents on July 8 he could fully determine his ground.

From May until the day Jewett expected the regents to take action on the report of the special committee, he furtively and most indiscreetly sought to influence public opinion on behalf of the library plan. Thus to George Livermore he wrote,

15 June 1854

My DEAR SIR,

I rec^d a few days ago, your kind note informing me that you had seen Mr. Hale, sen. about the republication of the article in the Advertiser & communicating his answer. I send today by Mr Cowles, the article somewhat corrected, to be reprinted by my brother. I should esteem it a great favor if you would look over the proofsheets. I have written to my brother that I had requested you to do so. If inconsistent with your engagements or your health, my brother will himself attend to it.

I have requested him to be *secretive* about the whole affair. It is very necessary that any connection of myself with it should not be made known or be traceable.

Pray take as many copies as you wish. I reprint it solely for gratuitous distribution.

I send to you by Mr Cowles a copy of the new edition of the catalogue system. I send one also for Mr Folsom. I shall have more copies in a few days.

There is nothing new here. I am very hard at work preparing for the 8th of July & I beg that this may be my excuse for so hasty a note.

I remain
ever truly yours[2]

[2]Original in the possession of Amos E. Jewett.

On July 8 the regents met, considered the special committee's report, and passed a resolution vesting the power to remove assistants in the secretary of the Institution. Backed by a majority opinion of the board, Henry summarily dismissed Jewett from his post, and after July 10 gave the library his personal supervision.

Jewett, it may well be imagined, was stunned, incredulous, at this momentous turn of events. He had worked against Henry's design to abandon and overturn the compromise resolutions, but always in the firm belief that in upholding the library plan he was championing the true intentions of the framers of the 1846 law. Possibly he did not realize how much his own personal interests and ego status had become identified with the defense of the library plan and propelled him along his unwise course. This blow shattered his illusions and brought him into the stark world of reality. Whether it induced a self-analysis of motivations is questionable. It is certain, however, that the shock of being dismissed, the blow to his pride, and the resultant notoriety deeply affected him, for while Jewett's was a proud nature, it was also a sensitive one. His faith in God, the devotion of his wife, and a fortitude drawn from the belief that he had acted in a manly way saved him from despair. The regents would meet in January, 1855. Choate would surely be there, as would Meacham, who was no admirer of Henry, and Stephen A. Douglas, who was partial to library interests. Vindication of his true course, as against what he regarded as Henry's underhanded methods, might come at their hands. Hopefully, Jewett rallied his spirits and awaited the outcome. It was truly pathetic, for all was already over with him in Washington, what with Henry, a large majority of the regents, and a great many congressmen being wholly sympathetic to the cause of science.

Secretary Henry had won the campaign, but battles were still in the offing. Jewett's removal touched off explosions in literary, scientific, and political circles. In Boston, for instance, sides were taken by the leading newspapers. The *Advertiser* championed Jewett, while the *Post,* the *Atlas,* and the *Journal* entered the lists for Henry. The noted astronomer, Benjamin Apthorp Gould, whose training in science quite naturally inclined him to take up the cudgels for Henry, contributed, over the initials "N. P. D.," six much-publicized articles to the *Post* during January and February of 1855 that were reprinted in pamphlet form. In these the newspapers that criticized Jewett's dismissal were mercilessly bombarded with facts. The *Advertiser* was taken to task for asserting that Jewett was fit for his post, that his dismissal was discourteous, that Henry's best friends admitted it to have been unnecessary and inexpedient, and that it was arbitrary and illegal—these in time became the stock arguments employed in Jewett's defense. Gould's rebuttals, which served a similar purpose on Henry's behalf, were that Jewett, while in charge of the library, had not even prepared a catalog of its holdings and had generally been remiss in the performance of his duties; that he had been insubordinate; and that his dismissal, termed "arbitrary, unjust and oppressive" by his supporters, had in fact been preceded by a majority vote of the regents, "the only object of which was to urge Professor Henry to a step already too long delayed, owing to his injudicious kind-liness of disposition."

Boston had no monopoly on the dramatic Smithsonian controversy. Everywhere pamphlets and periodical arti-cles treating of the matter were available in short order, speedily circulated, and avidly read. In the country at large, public opinion was divided as in the public prints. The *North American Review*, to which Livermore fre-quently contributed, deplored the abandonment of the library plan; *Norton's Literary Gazette* regarded the matter as settled conclusively by the dismissal of Jewett and called for the establishment of a national library at federal expense; the *Southern Literary Messenger* upheld the actions of Henry and the regents.

Meanwhile, the chief contestants were girding them-selves for the coming assault. At ten o'clock on the morn-ing of January 13, 1855, the regents held what must have been a highly argumentative and impassioned meeting. Choate, who had come from Boston to stand by Jewett, did his oratorical best. Henry, when called upon, ex-plained why he had found it necessary to remove Jewett, saying that he "deeply regretted the necessity" and giv-ing as his reasons the character of the paper submitted by Jewett to the special committe and the opinion of the committee in regard to that paper. The board, with some dissenting votes, to be sure, then approved the act of the secretary, likewise regretting its necessity. That day Choate took the step that brought on the final skir-mishes. He had left the Senate in March, 1845, but, be-cause of his interest in the library plan and his sympathy with Jewett's aims, he had remained upon the Board of Regents; he had recently been reappointed for a six-year term, although, from December, 1847, to May, 1854, he had not attended a single meeting. On January 13, to Jesse D. Bright, president *pro tempore* of the Senate, and to Linn Boyd, speaker of the House of Representatives, he addressed identical letters in which he resigned his position as regent. This dramatic action caused a profound sensation in Congress.

In the Senate a resolution was introduced, requesting that the Committee on the Judiciary inquire into the alleged violations of law by the regents and Secretary Henry. The committee concluded its business in a brief period, and in its report of February 6 unanimously sustained the course taken by the administration of the Institution as entirely legal.

In the House, where streams of sharp debates and floods of oratory were loosed, a select committee of five was appointed and moved apace to investigate the affairs of the Institution. The chairman, Charles W. Upham, of Massachusetts, who was from Jewett's boyhood town, and who later became known as the first scientific historian of the Salem witchcraft delusions, soon found himself bombarded with letters defending Jewett. Choate sent two warm letters upholding the library plan, and Meacham, Jewett's brother, John, George Livermore, and others hurried to lend support to the librarian's cause. These efforts were hardly necessary to convince Upham, as he was already in the Choate camp. Many who were not necessarily prolibrary, but rather against the current Smithsonian policies, sought to influence the committee. A vigorous editorial of January 20, in Greeley's powerful

93

New York Weekly Tribune, called for an overhauling of the institution which, with its "vicious system of publication," had served as "a sort of lying-in asylum for luxurious authors where their still-born offspring are arrayed in useless splendor at the expense of a fund given for no such purpose."

Henry did not lack defenders of influence and note. From Louis Agassiz, an intimate friend of the Secretary, and one whose contributions to science were universally acknowledged, and from Benjamin Peirce, Perkins professor of mathematics and astronomy at Harvard College, came strong letters approving his stand.

Both Henry and Jewett testified before the committee, frequently with emotion and mutual recriminations. After several meetings the committee terminated its hearings and the members, on March 3, submitted their "reports." The "majority" report, signed by the chairman, came out for the library plan, as might have been expected; two other members presented one dissenting from his, and the remaining members declined to sign either. Thus did the Smithsonian fracas die down and pass into legislative oblivion.

Jewett was furious. Yet he had no further recourse. His language well reflected his anger. Almost a month and a half after the House committee had "reported," he was still beside himself with rage as he wrote to Folsom, fulminating and denouncing the machinations of those who had laid him low.

You have doubtless been an interested spectator of recent movements concerning the miserable Smithsonian matter. The course pursued by Prof Henry & his partisans can be dictated only by desperation. The lying & ferocious attacks upon me, —the glaring frauds & outrageous misrepresentations & tricks respecting the report of the investigating committee, the assaults upon Mr. Choate, Mr Upham & all others who dare differ from them will recoil upon their heads. . . .[3]

Despite his personal feeling, however, he did not wish to see the work on the Library of Congress catalog cease. It may be that he only wished to have a club to hold over his "enemies" in the end. But, more probably, he had a genuine interest in the undertaking. Therefore, when Henry appointed Professor William E. Jillson, formerly of Brown University, to superintend the task, Jewett placed his advice and services at the latter's beck and call. Still, he could not help mourning rather melodramatically that he would not be able to complete the project himself:

. . . This work upon the Catalogue of the Library of Congress will probably conclude in the course of three or four months, the appropriation being exhausted & the preparation of the titles nearly or quite finished. It is the most painful & mortifying circumstance in connection with my present position that the malice & meanness of my enemies have prevailed to defeat & destroy this great literary project upon which I had bestowed so much time, toil & money, just at the moment when a few weeks longer continuance of my authority in regard to it would have placed it beyond their power. It makes me sick to think of it. . . .[4]

[3]To Charles Folsom, April 11, 1855, Folsom Papers, Boston Public Library.
[4]*Ibid.*

During the spring of 1855 Jewett cast about for possible employment. He was not wealthy, he had a family looking to him for support, and his wife was expecting another child. An offer of a teaching position at Harvard was tendered him, likewise the presidency of a western college. For a time he thought of taking a professorship at a college in Washington which was to be reorganized and opened that fall with ample funds. Still, he hoped devoutly for a librarianship worthy of his talents. In May he prepared to return to his native New England, being drawn back in part to arrange a family reunion which he and his brother John (somewhat affluent after having published *Uncle Tom's Cabin*) were planning. A circular, signed by himself and others, had already been sent to all known living members of the Jewett family in America, requesting them to attend a meeting at Rowley, Massachuetts, on June 14, to

give an opportunity for mutual conference, and joyful greetings, for renewing and strengthening the bonds of common brotherhood, and, in particular, to adopt measures for obtaining such historic facts as will perfect the genealogy of the Jewett family and perpetuate those facts by publication in a well printed and neatly bound volume.

And Charles Jewett, as the most widely known member of the family, had been chosen orator of the day. With a heavy heart and a fierce hatred of Henry, Jewett gathered his family together and turned his back upon Washington.

Departing from the city which had promised so much and failed him so miserably, he might well have bolstered his sagging faith with a perusal of his accomplishments during his more than six years of service at the Smithsonian Institution. What he had achieved did not seem small in its day to the interested and informed. He left an organized and developed library of thirty-two thousand volumes, with its vital records—accessions catalog and shelf list—in good shape. His historic survey of "public libraries" had set a standard for such compilations; his suggestions relative to copyright materials had been adopted in part by Congress; his rules for cataloging had been employed by several libraries in the preparation of their catalogs; and his advocacy of the 1853 Librarians' Convention had brought the nascent profession and some of its problems forcibly to public attention.

He failed at some tasks, but what he aimed to accomplish is worthy of consideration. To be sure, his finding list, his card catalog, and his supervision of the Smithsonian library in its later years, were not of the best. And the library itself—his most substantial labor—was transferred in 1866 to the Library of Congress.

Unfortunately, the project on which he had most set his heart was never to be crowned with complete success. The catalog of all books in Washington libraries, which he had initiated, as the first real step in the preparation of a union catalog of all libraries, was set aside in order that all effort might be concentrated on the perfection of the scheme for stereotyping the catalogs of libraries. This in turn had to be modified to the extent of being limited to the collection of the Library of Congress, and even that work was suspended after the first

97

part of the catalog had been issued. While expense was an important factor in its abandonment the real death blow to the project was administered by the clay blocks which showed themselves so subject to extreme shrinkage and warping during baking that, when baked, an exact adjustment of them on the press was impossible. After Jewett's departure the Smithsonian made a brave effort to carry on the stereotyping operations, but by November, 1856, "that mighty limbo of expensive ventures," as Henry Stevens labeled the Institution, had ceased all work on the Library of Congress catalog. Still, the stereotyping plan was to continue to prove stimulating to other minds, and, as late as 1888, Guido Biagi would translate Jewett's 1853 exposition of it into the Italian language, by order of Luigi Cremona, officer of bibliography to King Victor Emmanuel.

Apart from the librarians who were aware of the problems with which Jewett had grappled and who admired his bold and original efforts in seeking solutions, apart from the literary men and the partisans of the library plan who for obvious reasons defended his course, and apart from his close friends, probably few persons, in the spring of 1855, believed that Jewett had accomplished anything substantial or that his case merited more than a small amount of pity. No better summation of the popular point of view—that he had done little and that he deserved dismissal for inattention to duties and insubordination—may be found than in the articles which Benjamin A. Gould submitted to the *Boston Post* during the period when the controversy reached its peak in fury.

These contained certain damaging accusations which Jewett's defenders do not seem to have been able to refute. Gould's charges were based, in large part, not on hearsay or wild rumor, but on observations and investigations made largely by himself. Leveled as they were against Jewett's fitness for his position, they bear examination.

Gould claimed that Jewett had embarked upon a scheme for cataloging the books of the entire country when he had not even prepared a list, let alone a catalog, of the books belonging to the Smithsonian Institution itself, and further, that he had become so thoroughly absorbed in pushing the stereotyping scheme, and later in attacking Henry, that he had not sufficient time in which to attend to his library duties. Jewett and his supporters aimed to confute these statements by asserting that when Jewett was dismissed he left an accessions catalog and shelf list up to date in entries, a catalog of the books in the library on cards, and an alphabetical catalog of all the books and pamphlets in the library, with their shelf-location numbers on sheets (the finding list). This was grist for Gould's mill, and he made the most of it.

Gould stated emphatically that these records were incomplete and in chaotic condition. He recalled that in February, 1853,

. . . We had occasion for a book which we knew to be in the library, but after some hours spent in hunting for it, were compelled to abandon the search in despair. Shortly after, so strong a complaint was made that Mr. Jewett was in a manner compelled to have something prepared in the form of a list of the Smithsonian books.

99

He went on to point out that no regular list of all the books or pamphlets received by the Institution was ever fully kept, that the finding list consisted of sheets of paper on which were pasted strips with the names of various books, and that these sheets listed only the materials on two of the four sides of the library hall, and did not contain the titles of those received by exchange —a number larger than those purchased. Moreover, said he, Jewett had allowed assistants to compile the list of publications received without adequate supervision, and he proceeded to give as examples some of the titles on the list exactly as he had found them entered: under the heading 'Poetry', "J. M. Harris, *Shrubs of Alabama*" and "Stowe, H. B. *Key to Uncle Tom's Cabin*"; under 'Philosophical and Astronomical School Books', "Fulton and Eastman, *Book-keeping*." He drove home the fact that two thirds of the shelves and all of the cases in the library hall were not lettered or numbered until after Jewett had left, and that although a few cards had been prepared toward beginning a catalog, these never comprised more than one quarter of the books in the library.

"More has been done toward arranging the lists and books, in the six months since Mr. Jewett went," he added, "than had been done in the seven years of his connection with the library." There were other charges, among them that Jewett had paid, during the political struggle involving the mayoral position, for the insertion of articles "to prejudice the Washington public" against the incumbent, Maury. Gould did his best to pulverize the refutations of what he termed the "Jewett-Meacham movement" partisans. While some of the arrows of ac-

100

cusation fell heavily to the ground, others clearly hit their mark.

What had transpired may easily be surmised. Jewett, absorbed in the stereotyping scheme, had allowed many routine functions to be handled through the procedures he had early drawn up. He did not have the true faculty of administration, and, once involved with the projects, let the daily work go along unsupervised. He disliked detailed routines, although when he toiled in his own channel and upon his own projects, no detail was too small to merit consideration. By the middle of 1853 he had thrown himself so completely into the Library of Congress catalog labor, that he could no longer see the forest for the trees. He was hopelessly involved.

To insure this work's success, for on it hinged the execution of the entire elaborate stereotyping system and so many of his future plans, he had to move quickly. Projects were jettisoned and the Congressional library catalog became the work of the hour. Hardly had it begun when Jewett's chief assistant left the service for reasons of health. In this contingency Jewett decided to concentrate his forces on the Library of Congress job, to abandon the cataloging of the Smithsonian library books on cards, and to have the titles written out on slips of paper just before they were to be printed for a projected stereotyped catalog of the library. The finding list was purposely made brief, because it was a temporary tool, since the library was soon expected to be removed to the main building. It was a case of doing too much in one direction and too little in another. Of course he may have had to put many things aside because he suffered from having so small a staff. He himself stated later that, though he received an annual salary of but $2,500, and his two assistants $600 and $540 respectively, he was compelled on more than one occasion to pay other assistants out of his own pocket. This, of course, was his undertaking. Henry had never asked him to keep so many projects going at one time, nor so thoroughly to engage his aids on one project that work could not be carried on competently on any of the others, or, indeed, to hire assistants to relieve him of duties he felt beneath his position. All these elements, if they did not serve to make defeat more certain, at least made for a sad condition of affairs by July, 1854. At that goal more often sought than attained—*aurea mediocritas*—librarian Jewett did not, indeed could not by nature, aim, and thus unwittingly he provided his "enemies" with a liberal supply of ammunition for their cannonades against his efficiency, his compliance with duty, and even his discretion.

Yet, it should be remembered, the various charges and counter claims were made during the heat of battle, a time when words and phrases such as "defalcation," "perversion of trust," and "faithlessness" were being bandied about. It seems hardly possible that Henry, "his injudicious kindliness" aside, would have kept a man on his staff who was the rather incompetent individual Gould has drawn up for posterity. And it is more remarkable that a library in so chaotic a state would have been open to the public with no loud criticism forthcoming, that so trained an observer as Willard Fiske, who visited the library during the identical year and season as Gould did, should have noticed nothing lax or slovenly in techniques, and that men like Folsom, Haven, and Hale would have been content to be led in a national convention by an irresponsible individual. It is difficult to believe that a librarian of Jewett's competence would have allowed his library to go to pieces around him without caring or giving some attention to its plight. A man of his experience must surely have had more perception and conscience than Gould would have us think. That he was absorbed in projects is true, that he gambled too much on the stereotyping scheme is proved, but that he was incompetent must be accepted with great reservation.

On one count, however, there can be neither refutation nor palliation. It was insubordination that laid Jewett low. He was a man who, without doubt, knew how to get along with his assistants and his colleagues. He knew how to give orders—though he was not especially inclined toward administration. Whether he was willing to take orders from others in this period is open to question. He was an individual who had to be free at all times to exercise initiative without restraint. Henry had early realized this and allowed him independence—too much, perhaps—in handling library affairs. Despite the hands-off policy of the Secretary (he does not seem to have interfered with Jewett or his work), it was not long before Jewett became restive under his general direction and grew impatient with the restraints of a subordinate position.

The seed of misunderstanding was sown when Jewett was appointed by the Board of Regents to the staff of the Institution in a way that led him to believe himself the independent head of a department and the policy maker for that department. The real rub came with the compromise resolutions which the Regents probably ought never have adopted. These, to be sure, were regarded at the time of their adoption as a means of reconciling the different views of the members of the board in order that the major functioning of the Institution might begin. They were not conceived as the basis of a permanent, long-range program; they were measures expedient and temporary. But Jewett was induced to consider them otherwise because of the manner of his appointment, his friendship with the "literary men" and the partisans of the library plan, and his natural interest in furthering the concerns of the library. He felt honor-bound to carry the library banner before the crowd and to rally supporters from all sides. Although his ideas about bringing the library plan into complete operation were not those entertained by his superior (and, it later developed, by a majority of the regents), he pursued his own course, and endeavored to defeat Henry's efforts to annul the compromise agreement by every possible means. Certainly he laid himself open to the charge of insubordination.

Henry and Jewett operated on different principles. Because of his previous training and accomplishments in science, Henry inclined to the view that the institution for which Smithson had provided in his will and which bore his name should stress one field of knowledge—science. On this ground he was in agreement with the Board of Regents as a whole, with the majority of the members of Congress, and, it would appear, with the people of the country at large. The partisans of the library plan, however, were relatively small in number. But they had a strong champion in Jewett, who looked confidently to the future of the Smithsonian as a national library. Until 1854 he probably derived comfort from the fact that there was a divergence of views about the library plan among the Board of Regents, and that that body had not put an end to the compromise resolutions. But when the matter came under consideration, instead of waiting hopefully for a possible nod from the regents —for who could tell but that Henry's efforts to have the compromise arrangement rescinded might fail and the report of the special committee be rejected?—he instantly donned his armor.

With Henry and Jewett championing opposite principles from the beginning of their association, and both determined to see their respective principles become the chief policy of the Institution, the ground was well prepared for the regrettable personal clash that came. It was made all the more inevitable by Jewett who, it would seem, allowed his experience at Brown University, the praise he had received for his work there, and his national reputation to go to his head. He got somewhat highhanded with Henry before they ceased speaking to one another, and assumed an irritating air of superiority toward the Secretary that only served to speed up the approaching day of reckoning. During the last years of their attempted cooperation, his conduct toward Henry was frequently offensive and insulting. Still, the disagreement between the two men stemmed first from principles and second from temperament. Through the years both factors merged to the point of being indistinguishable. Henry, by 1855, was in his fifties, a man settled in mind, firm in his beliefs; in controversy resolute, unyielding, and controlled. Jewett, a younger man (in his late thirties), was daring and impulsive, mercurial in temperament, and as tenacious of belief as Henry; such was his nature, however, that he could not help becoming impassioned in contention and savage in battle. That Jewett was more to blame than Henry in the controversy, and that Henry's views on the future function of the Smithsonian as a bulwark of scientific knowledge were the more foresighted and wise, the most impartial observer must concede. However, had the regents, in 1846 and 1847, defined precisely the operations of the Institution, the unfortunate conflict might never have come about.[5]

[5]Reuben A. Guild, Jewett's friend and eulogistic biographer, covering up for the sake of posterity, insisted in his "Memorial Sketch of Prof. C. C. Jewett" that "there was no personal hostility between the Secretary and Assistant Secretary," a statement that does not stand up upon a reading of the hearings before the House committee of 1855, at which both men denounced each other freely. And, if additional evidence be needed, it comes in a letter from Justin Winsor to Herbert Baxter Adams, dated April 18, 1888 (Adams Papers, Johns Hopkins University Library), in which Winsor recalled:

... You know that the fight over the future of the Smithsonian was fought at the beginning of its existence, by Henry with a majority of the Trustees on the side of Science, and C. C. Jewett then the ass't secy with Rufus Choate as a helper on the side of literature; and that Science beat. It caused an enmity between Henry and Jewett; and I remember when I succeeded Jewett as Supt. of the Boston Public Library, I recd a letter from Henry, hoping that I was not an inheritor officially of Jewett's antagonism to him; and that our relations would be friendly, as they were . . . .

IX

A New Path Opens

IT IS NOT EASY to fix a date for the first suggestion of a public library in the city of Boston. The idea was entertained from time to time by many citizens. Proposals for combining some of the social libraries of the metropolis to form one institution open to the general public had been advanced occasionally after the turn of the eighteenth century, but without success. In 1840, Alexandre Vattemare, while seeking to stir up support for his international book-exchange system during a tour of the land, came to Boston. Finding here, as he had been pained to discover in other localities, no public institution capable of receiving the objects he expected to exchange, he immediately set about arousing enthusiasm for a public library. Meetings of citizens followed, and resolutions looking to the end agreed upon were passed. But hardly had Vattemare departed for Europe when the fever died down, and nothing further was accomplished. In 1843, however, the city of Boston received a number of valuable books from the Municipal Council of Paris, in return for a present of books it had donated to the French body through the efforts of Vattemare. It was a harbinger of good. Within a few years the intrepid Frenchman returned to America and to Boston, where he employed his most persuasive talents in inducing Mayor Josiah

Quincy, Jr., to initiate legislation requesting the permission of the Commonwealth of Massachusetts to tax the citizens of Boston for the support of a public library. On April 3, 1848, the city of Boston accepted such an authorization act passed by the state legislature. Several unsuccessful endeavors were made to establish the desired institution, one seeking to make the exclusive Athenaeum its basis. These efforts were given additional impetus when word came that John Jacob Astor, the wealthiest man in America, had died, leaving a large bequest for laying the foundations of a public library in New York City. Shortly thereafter, gentlemen of wealth and prestige began to donate money or portions of their personal library collections to the city, which had appointed a public library committee of the council. In 1849 Robert C. Winthrop presented a selection of bound United States government publications, and in that year Samuel A. Eliot and others also gave books. The following year Mayor John P. Bigelow contributed $1,000 and Edward Everett, former president of Harvard University, offered the collection of public documents he had accumulated in his many years of government service, these numbering upwards of a thousand volumes. It was not long before a modest collection of books had been gathered in an upper room of the City Hall set aside for their deposit. The books were not allowed to circulate, and "little use was made of them on the premises." By 1851 these amounted to some two thousand volumes, and, by 1852, to slightly less than four thousand.

In February, 1852, Mayor Benjamin Seaver called the attention of the city government to the subject of the formation of a public library. He suggested that "rooms easy of access in a central part of the city be secured," that a librarian be appointed, and that a board of trustees be elected. The trustees were to report "upon the objects to be obtained by the establishment of a public library and the means of effecting them." Seaver's suggestions were acted upon favorably. On July 6 the "preliminary" report of the Trustees was submitted to the City Council.

This historic document traced the growth of the library movement up to that day and stated fully the reasons for the establishment of the library. It pointed out that a public library was needed to supplement the work of the public schools by granting free access to books and also to enable graduates of the schools to continue their "pursuit of knowledge." It emphasized that libraries "owned by private corporations" were not able, by reason of their proprietorship, to assume the role of a public library. It set forth the classes of books to be contained in the collection and advocated in clear and unmistakable language the "revolutionary" plan of free and unrestricted circulation of books, a plan conforming, in the main, with Ticknor's firm belief that

. . . not only the best books of all sorts, but the pleasant literature of the day, should be made accessible to the whole people at the only time when they care for it, i.e. when it is fresh and new. . . .

Everett, Dr. Nathaniel Shurtleff, and other members of the Board had grave misgivings about such doctrines and hoped for a municipal reference and research library. But Ticknor, by the greatest exertion and eloquence, dragged them to the mark and himself wrote the major portion of the liberal paper. In their report the trustees suggested that the rooms on the ground floor of the Adams schoolhouse on Mason Street be granted for use of the library.

By one of the fortunate turns of fate, a copy of this report fell into the hands of Joshua Bates, a member of the banking house of Baring Brothers & Company, London, to which company the city of Boston, endeavoring to negotiate for a waterworks construction loan, had submitted various documents, among them the report on the public library. Bates, on leafing through the report, could not help recalling his early days as a youth in Boston, where, often without money to pay for fire or light in his rooms, he passed many an evening reading in the bookshop of Hastings, Etheridge & Bliss, thanks to the kindness of the proprietors. If only there had been a public library in those days where a young man might have had the opportunity of improving his mind and profitably passing his leisure hours! True humanitarian zeal, combined with grateful remembrance of the acts of kindness he had received in Boston, prompted him to make a most liberal offer. Struck by the idea of a public library as an adjunct to the public school system, he wrote Mayor Seaver of his willingness to give $50,000 to the city for the purchase of books for a public library, with the proviso that the city itself construct a building and take care of all expenses.

Needless to say, Bates' offer was accepted. The trustees requested him to allow his donation to be funded and only the interest expended for the purchase of books, and to this he cheerfully consented. Meanwhile, a librarian, Edward Capen, having been appointed, all necessary preparations were made for setting up the library in what were regarded as provisional headquarters in Mason Street. On March 20, 1854, the doors of the Boston Public Library opened for the first time to welcome the citizens of the city to a reading room. Three months later (May 2) the circulation of books began. Before the library closed for the annual examination of books (October 17), 6,590 persons had passed through its portals to register for privileges and to withdraw for home use 35,389 volumes. In less than half a year the library had proved its worth.

The library then occupied two rooms on the ground floor of the Mason Street building, an outer room and an inner, or "library" room. In the outer room, which served as the reading room, were available for consultation some 138 periodicals and transactions of mechanics' institutes and scientific bodies. Upon the tables were printed copies of an alphabetical catalog, in which were listed the titles of the books in the collection; on blank interleaves the titles of current acquisitions were noted. For want of space, the reading room, with an average daily attendance of three hundred persons, was also used for the delivery of books; and, as a result, noise filled a room which should have been dedicated to quiet reading. The "library room" was small, poorly lighted, ill-ventilated, cold in winter, and soon became so crowded with books that it was almost impossible to find space for incoming acquisitions.

In November, 1854, the city council adopted an ordinance appointing commissioners to plan the erection of a library building. Bates, informed in 1855 that construction of a building on Boylston Street was in progress, wrote Ticknor and Everett in July of his desire to give a large quantity of books to fill up the shelves of the new edifice. He asked only that there be made out and forwarded to him "a Catalogue of French, German and Italian Books, and such English works as are most needed, the whole not to exceed in cost $20,000 or $30,000." As Bates had requested the cooperation of the trustees, it now fell to their lot to draw up the "Catalogue" for transmission to London. Ticknor immediately began to collect lists of the most desirable books from such distinguished men in different parts of the country as Professor Louis Agassiz, Brigadier-General Sylvanus Thayer of the United States Army, and Judge Benjamin R. Curtis of the United States Supreme Court.

All told, he and the trustees applied to more than fifty eminent men in the fields of science, literature, law, philosophy, and the fine arts, as well as to engineers, architects, clergymen, and officials in the armed forces of the nation. From these gentlemen came "kind" and ample answers. As the lists began to pour in it became obvious that some selection of the titles thereon would have to be made. The trustees later noted:

. . . The task of selecting, from the almost boundless mass of literature, ancient and modern, in our own and foreign tongues, those works which it would be expedient to recommend to our liberal benefactor for immediate purchase, was not to be performed without reflection and labor. . . .

For aid in this task the trustees now turned to "Charles C. Jewett, Esq." who had been appointed by them in June, 1855, "to assist in arranging the card catalogue and preparing a system for its continuation."

Jewett had left Washington, the scene of the Smithsonian turbulence, a saddened and bitterly disappointed man. The whole affair involving his dismissal had been painful and humiliating, and had caused him no end of suffering. Yet, withal, it was to have a salutary effect, for from it he would learn much. Upon his arrival in Massachusetts, and maybe before, Jewett, hoping for congenial employment, had apparently turned to friends and literary men sympathetic with his plight and familiar with the range of his abilities: to George Livermore, influential in literary circles, to Edward Everett, one of the 1850 commissioners to examine the stereotyping plan, and to George Ticknor, whom he had known as early as 1847 and whose interests in European literature somewhat paralleled his own. On June 12 the Board of Trustees of the Boston Public Library had authorized its president, Everett, together with Ticknor and Shurtleff, to employ Jewett on the cataloging labors of the institution.

Two days later, possibly with the offer of the trustees at hand, Jewett had attended the Jewett reunion at Rowley, Massachusetts, to which had come about six hundred members of the family from fourteen states of the Union. As a holiday had been declared in the town and school let out, thousands of people had turned out to see the procession of Jewetts through Rowley to the old Jewett homestead (a house taken down in 1875), where various speeches had been made. Then all had repaired to church

113

where, in the course of the services, Charles Coffin Jewett had delivered an oration in which he "urged the young Jewetts to take example from the valor, virtue, learning and integrity of their fathers." The day had ended with a sumptuous dinner.

By June 21 Jewett had accepted the offer of the trustees and soon after entered upon his duties. On July 8 his wife, to his great joy, presented him with a son, Charles Sidney. The picture was brightening considerably, for as it chanced, at the very time that Jewett began his work on the catalogs of the public library, Bates was writing to Everett and Ticknor concerning his second donation to the institution. It was not long after that the trustees informed Jewett of their desire for his services in selecting the titles for the list to be forwarded to Bates.

Jewett fell to work with fervor, preparing the required "Catalogue" or, rather, the list of titles. For more than two months he labored incessantly, eight hours a day, in the spacious library of Ticknor's home on Park Street, one of the largest and best-selected private libraries in all New England. Jewett's "bibliographical pursuits" and experiences in purchasing books in Europe for Brown University stood him in good stead. Every available bibliographical tool was consulted, every source was pumped dry. The first task was to write on separate slips of paper each of the titles furnished by the men whom Ticknor and the other trustees had consulted. These slips were then arranged in alphabetical order, duplicate titles and those already in the catalog of the library in Mason Street were rejected, and the titles revised, where necessary, by consulting catalogs and bibliographical dictionaries. The best edition of each book was selected and jotted down on the slip, together with notes which would guide the purchasers in Europe. In these endeavors Jewett had the active aid and cooperation of Ticknor. It must have been a happy collaboration. Ticknor knew books and the state of book markets in America and Europe. In earlier years he had traveled widely throughout Europe and from its book marts had purchased some of the thousands of volumes he needed in order to write his monumental history of Spanish literature. At home he always kept upon his table, for frequent study, the catalogs of books for sale at auction, as well as those issued by publishers and booksellers. After about thirty-five thousand volumes had been selected by himself and Jewett, the slips were sorted "with reference to the economy and convenience of purchasing," and separate lists written out and successively dispatched to Bates in London for approval. Bates, in turn, transmitted them to agents in London, Paris, Leipzig, and Florence, where they were given immediate attention. In May, 1856, the speed with which his agents had moved was evidenced by the arrival in Boston of the first boxes of Bates books, addressed to the Public Library of Boston.

The trustees realized, by 1855, that not only was there insufficient accommodation in the rooms in Mason Street for the ever-increasing library collection (some volumes, indeed, had been removed and deposited temporarily in the Quincy schoolhouse), but there was no space in which to receive and prepare the Bates volumes for use. That these specific purposes might be better accomplished, they leased a house in Boylston Place, near the site of the new library building, in December of that year, and, granting Jewett the services of a few assistants, placed him in sole charge of these combined operations.

It was not a light task. The number of books alone was staggering. By October, 1857, some 142 cases containing 21,374 volumes had been received. Their cost touched the then astronomical figure of $38,893; with the passage of time the sum would soar past $50,000. The labor entailed in the reception of the books and their preparation for the shelves caused Jewett to organize the equivalent of an acquisition and cataloging department. He outlined his procedures with great care, so that each volume, after having been compared with the invoice, went through successive steps of collation, entry in the accessions catalog, cataloging, and classification.

Rather thorough cataloging was done, each volume being entered on a card, with full title, "accurate designations of authorship, edition, form and number of volumes, and occasional bibliographical notes." The contents of all the collected works of an author were given in full, as were the contents of collections of single works by various authors published with a common title. Every work of every author appeared under his name; cross references were made for every word of the title under which it was likely that a reader might look for the work in either an alphabetical or a classified index. Jewett hoped, by including such details, to prevent the purchase of duplicates of titles that might be buried in collections and to relieve librarians and readers of inconvenience and loss of time. Each volume was also cataloged on slips, with a short title and such information as would correspond to that found in the printed catalog of the library in Mason Street. Jewett thought these slips might be used in the future for printing a short-title catalog of the library, without the necessity of re-examining the volumes once they had left his hands and found their way to the shelves.

In accounting for the numerous processes through which every book had to pass, Jewett called attention to the fact that once the work had been done in so thorough a manner, it was done "for all time." Furthermore, all the materials would exist

. . . for the rapid and easy preparation and publication of *any kind* of catalogue which may be demanded,—with long titles or with short titles; alphabetical, chronological, or classed; with separate indexes of subjects, or with such indexes combined in one alphabet, with the authors and titles. . . .

Because the library building was not yet completed, it was necessary to defer the assigning of a specific location for each book on the shelves, the preparation of the shelf lists, in which their order on the shelves would be recorded, and "the marking of the number of the shelf and the order of the book upon the book itself." As each box of books was processed, it was repacked and removed to the basement of the Boylston Street building.

In the performance of his duties, Jewett brought to bear his characteristic enthusiasm and energy. By 1856 he had put the Washington trouble behind him. His mind was settled and at peace—save when thoughts of Henry intruded upon his consciousness. He was particularly pleased with his situation in the library, which he found consistent with his interests and congenial to his tastes. The preparation of the lists for Bates seemed an Elysian occupation, so grateful was he that he could work far away from strife. He deeply appreciated the opportunity to work once again in quiet surroundings where he could feel that he was "doing something to good purpose." All the while, his good efforts and well-ordered work were neither unobserved nor unappreciated by the trustees. His labors were not to go unrewarded.

In the early days of the library (1852), when it became apparent that someone was needed to care for the constant accumulation of books sent in by donors to the assigned room in the City Hall, the city council decided to appoint a librarian. There were three or four candidates, among them Samuel G. Drake, the noted antiquarian, who held out as an inducement for his election to the post "that the library should receive *his* valuable library of Americana."[1] The council had not been impressed, and Edward Capen, secretary of the Boston School Committee, had been appointed. Capen had proved a capable librarian and had presided over affairs in Mason Street with good effect. By 1856, however, the trustees anticipated a large increase in the use of the library, once it began operations in the new building. It followed that procedures in its various departments would have to be enlarged, that the direction of the library would become more exacting, and that a reorganization of its administration would be necessary. While the collection of popular books in Mason Street

[1]Edward Capen, to Justin Winsor, January 31, 1882, Winsor Papers, Massachusetts Historical Society.

118

had, to be sure, been successfully cared for under Capen, there was need for the organization of the higher class of books being received from Bates. To administer thoroughly both collections would require giving the chief control of the library "to a skilled hand."

On November 2, 1857, the trustees presented a memorial to the city council urging the establishment of the position of superintendent of the library. They referred to the arduous work required in the circulation department, as well as the labor necessary in cataloging and preparing for circulation more than six thousand books annually, and called attention to the expected increase in these functions. They enumerated, among the qualifications for the position, the ability "to prepare judiciously and with discrimination, the requisite selected lists of books to be purchased annually at home and abroad, and an extensive knowledge of books, of ancient and foreign languages, and of science and literature generally." In addition to having bibliographical and technical ability, said they, the superintendent would have to be, for the competent management and administration of this type of growing institution,

. . . an efficient and responsible head, possessing a degree of ability and qualifications, intellectual and literary, of a higher order than can be expected on the part of young persons of either sex, however intelligent, who perform services of routine for a moderate compensation. . . .

On January 1, 1858, the library building on Boylston Street was dedicated with public ceremonies attended by a large crowd. The following day a city ordinance was passed, establishing the office of superintendent of the public library. It required that the trustees nominate a person for the office and pass the nomination on to the city council, which would itself elect the superintendent. Jewett, however, was promptly recommended by trustees Edward Everett, Oliver Frost, and William W. Greenough, who stressed his wide experience, his eminent qualifications, and the excellence of his work under the direction of the book committee of the trustees for more than two years. Nor did they fail to add that "Professor Jewett enjoys the personal confidence of Mr. Bates." His election was a foregone conclusion. The council speedily confirmed his appointment, at an annual salary of $2000.

Jewett could have asked for no more fitting reward for his many years of service in libraries, nor for a more complete vindication of his abilities as a librarian. Here, at last, was an uncommon opportunity for doing work "to good purpose" and for the exercise, so important to his nature, of that initiative. Many persons across the country probably wondered whether he would not soon become the center of as dramatic a furor with the trustees as he had with Henry. There was, however, a fine theoretical distinction between his positions in Washington and Boston, a distinction which a man of his temperament readily appreciated. In Washington he had been subordinate to Henry, who was himself responsible to the Board of Regents; in Boston he was to have sole command and to answer for his work, not to an intermediary, but directly to the Board of Trustees.

X

Superintendent Jewett Takes Hold

JEWETT TOOK HOLD of the position of superintendent of
the Public Library of Boston at an auspicious time. During the decade of the fifties there was, throughout the
country, an "infectious interest" in books that best mani-
fested itself in the establishment of several large and
important public libraries. The Astor Library in New
York, like the Boston Public Library, opened its doors in
1854; three years later the Peabody Institute of Baltimore
was founded. Under Joseph Green Cogswell's guiding
hand the growth of the Astor Library was especially
rapid. By the summer of 1858 the shelves held more
than a hundred thousand volumes, of such range and
quality that Cogswell could write that Buckle, the English historian, might well have penned his *History of
Civilization* by using its resources. There was as yet no
completely accurate count of public libraries in the
United States, but the Eighth Census (1860) would soon
report the existence of more than ten thousand public
libraries, possessing in the aggregate some eight million
volumes. These figures did not include another eight
million volumes in the collections of school and Sunday-
school libraries.

Jewett was to direct the course of an institution that
contained, in 1858, some seventy thousand volumes, an

impressive number. Already, the Public Library of Boston had forged ahead of most of the longer-established libraries in America. It surpassed, in holdings, the Library of Congress (50,700) and the Library Company of Philadelphia (64,900); and it ranked alongside the Boston Athenaeum (70,000). Only the Astor Library and Harvard, which stood first in the country with some 112,000 volumes, could match its size.

Following his appointment as superintendent, Jewett continued to supervise the preparation of the Bates volumes on Boylston Place, and to engage in "other occupations connected with the library and its catalogues." After February 1, the new library building being ready for occupancy, the Bates volumes were removed from Boylston Place to the upper hall. There, they and the books that had been stored in the basement, those which had been on deposit in the Quincy schoolhouse, and some that "could best be spared from the rooms in Mason Street," were, under Jewett's direction, provisionally classified and arranged. By the beginning of August, all the books in Mason Street having been transferred to Boylston Street, the library closed its rooms at the Adams schoolhouse.

Apparently a broad division of duties between the superintendent and the librarian, previously outlined by the trustees, now went into effect. Capen assumed charge of the circulation of books and affairs in the lower hall, a general circulation department of popular books on the first floor of the edifice corresponding to that which he had previously directed. Jewett was entrusted with the general supervision of the entire institution, including both the lower and upper halls. His disinclination toward administrative work, for which he had limited capacity and patience, moved him to make short work of the matter by allowing Capen to administer his department relatively undisturbed. He himself undertook the supervision of the upper hall activities, the drawing up of lists of foreign books, particularly of the standard literature of the past, and instructions to the foreign and domestic agents of the library, as well as the arrangement and cataloging of the books. To the two latter tasks he early devoted the major portion of his time, both because he was partial to them and because he believed they constituted the most important part of his work. As superintendent he was made accountable to the trustees for the work of twenty-two persons, including himself and Capen, eleven male and eight female assistants, and a janitor.

Jewett's preoccupation with the arrangement and cataloging of books meant continuance of the work he had been engaged upon since 1855. No sooner had the Mason Street collection been transferred than he embarked upon a project—preparing an index to the catalog of the books to be shelved in the lower hall. There had been discussions about the feasibility of printing a "large and imposing" catalog of the entire library collection by 1858, and Jewett had initiated his elaborate cataloging procedures with such a work in mind. Ticknor had urged the preparation of a separate index to the books of the lower hall before any complete, printed catalog of the library should be attempted, and his view had prevailed. Jewett eagerly took hold of the project which Ticknor had proposed. Little time was lost during the transfer of the books to the new building. Extra assistants were employed; the Mason Street catalog was thoroughly revised, and, from it, short titles of books and a list of subjects were prepared. By September 17, 1858, when the reading room was opened, the printing of the index was under way. In December there came from the press the first copies of the *Index to the Catalogue of a Portion of the Public Library of the City of Boston Arranged in the Lower Hall*. With this volume at hand, the public circulation of books from the lower hall began on December 20.

Jewett, an inveterate believer in the subject approach in catalogs, had produced here a work of admirable scope and daring novelty. He had informed the trustees in 1858 that

. . . to constitute an army, the men must be organized for warlike operations. So, to form a library, books and titles must be rightly ordered for their appropriate use. . . .

So militant a theory did not suffer in practice. The *Index* contained a brief entry under the name of the author, together with the place and date of publication and the size of the book. Some fifteen thousand volumes were analyzed in its 204 pages. Each volume was also entered under a subject heading and again under the first prominent word of the title. Cross references were provided. All the entries—author, subject, and title—were arranged in one alphabet, a distinctly original departure from custom. Lest some should criticize the lack of bibliographical detail, Jewett took pains to emphasize that this volume was an index to the catalog, not the catalog itself. It was to serve as a simple and easy-to-use guide to the lower hall collection and nothing more. He pointed out that there was always a card catalog available for consultation by those seeking additional information about the indexed titles.

The favorable reception accorded the *Index* encouraged work upon a counterpart for the upper hall collection—a labor which had been begun before December, 1858. By 1861, that even more monumental volume had emerged from the press. The publication of the *Index to the Catalogue of Books in the Upper Hall of the Public Library of the City of Boston* heralded a new day for library catalogs. In scope, in comprehensiveness, in execution, it surpassed any similar compilation to which Jewett had put his hand. It was, according to Justin Winsor, "the most advanced specimen of library cataloguing which had then been produced in America."

Constructed upon the same principles as that of 1858, it disclosed the contents of some fifty-five thousand volumes. A dictionary arrangement was again employed, and cross references were liberally distributed throughout. Within its 902 pages books were recorded, not only under the names of their authors, but in brief form and without imprint, under subject headings, and often, too, under important catchwords of the titles. A system of classification ran through "the whole grouping of the titles by subjects." The general principle followed was to place books under the most specific subjects indicated by the titles and to make no references from specific to general headings. All books listed by author were not necessarily referred to by subject, for under subject headings Jewett took no notice of any work that did not fill a complete volume. Thus, a treatise by Francis Lieber, which did not make a single volume, would be found only under "Lieber, Francis," where there would be a full and exact note of the contents of his collected writings.

The *Index* contained a unique feature: an alphabetical analysis of the sessional papers of the British Parliament and Congressional documents of the United States designed to make immediately available more than three thousand volumes of valuable reports and discussions that it had usually taken researchers a great deal of time to ferret out for lack of a compact and convenient guide. It did not aim to be a complete index to all the public documents of England and America, but only to the most important ones that might frequently be called for in libraries. Still, the portion devoted to the parliamentary papers occupied fourteen pages with double columns (in pearl type), cost almost two months' labor on the part of the entire *Index* force, and was "the most complete (and perhaps the only complete) condensed index" to these papers then in existence.

While the *Index* contained pamphlet entries for authors "important enough," it did not attempt to examine the contents of the transactions of learned societies, as these were consulted by too few readers to make the effort worth while and there were already in the library satisfactory guides by Reuss and others to their materials. Besides, the sets in the library were far from complete. Because they were too voluminous, because most of them had "copious and well arranged" indexes, and because Poole's *Index*, the second edition of which had been published in 1853, covered the most important ones, periodicals were ignored.

The 1861 *Index* had been framed with the hope that its general features would be useful to libraries throughout the country. But local use was also considered. For the specific information of Boston patrons certain entries were starred; a single star denoted a volume available for circulation with permission, a double star signified one usable in the building but not subject to home loan.

Letters of praise and commendation upon the publication of the *Index* reached flood tide. From Henry Stevens in London, from Daniel Coit Gilman at Yale University, from librarians like Samuel Foster Haven and Lloyd P. Smith, and from scholars came congratulations, not only to Jewett, but to Ticknor and Everett who had encouraged his efforts. Joseph Green Cogswell, whose forte was the compilation of catalogs, wrote Jewett:

. . . Your Catalogue as far as it goes, comes up to my idea of what a Catalogue should be, that is a Dictionary of all that a library contains in a combined alphabet both of authors & subjects; if it could be carried out fully it would leave nothing to be desired for coming at a perfect knowledge of the contents of a library either by the librarian & his assistants or by readers. You have made a mighty stride toward the result. . . .[1]

How well Jewett's work stood up upon closer examination and longer use was the subject of another of Cogswell's letters, more than a year later, this time to Ticknor:

. . . When you see Mr. Jewett please say to him that I have

[1]September 21, 1861, Slips, Letters, etc. [Relating to the Administration of the Library], Boston Public Library.

availed myself of his labours very freely and hope he will not proceed against me for infringing his copyright. This use of his catalogue enables me to bear testimony to its unequalled excellence; it is a better key to the contents of the Library which it catalogues than any one in existence and how so much labour, resulting in nearly all the knowledge which a catalogue can impart and marked throughout by such wonderful correctness could have been accomplished in so short a time is quite miraculous. I do not believe the public are aware how much they are indebted to him.[2]

From Cambridge, President Cornelius Conway Felton of Harvard found time, while pursuing his onerous duties, to communicate to Everett his judgment of the volume:

. . . I have examined it with special care and have often consulted it for information, both in reference to subjects and writers. I consider it one of the most valuable books in my possession, independent of its utility to one who habitually uses the city library. I refer to it in my daily studies, and in connection with our College Library, and always with advantage. As a general index to literature, it is invaluable.[3]

And the Boston newspapers, in a glow of civic pride, commented in boastful terms upon the excellence of both indexes in bringing before the public the resources of the library.

By 1865 public demand from libraries and individuals would make necessary the printing of a second edition of the 1861 volume, which, in time, would prove the model for catalogs issued by the Mercantile Libraries of Brooklyn and Philadelphia and the library of the Uni-

[2]Copy of part of a letter to Ticknor, December 25, 1862, *ibid.*
[3]To Edward Everett, November 25, 1861, *ibid.*

versity of Leyden in Holland, among other institutions.

With the successful culmination of his endeavors on the index-catalogs, Jewett felt free to consider at length some troublesome problems of policy and administration. The compilation of supplements to both he could well afford to leave largely in the able hands of the two men whose assistance had contributed immeasurably to the merits of the volumes: Frederic Vinton, who had entered the service in 1856 as assistant to Capen and was well versed in classification; and William E. Jillson, librarian of the Patent Office, in Washington, who had aided Jewett during his summer vacations of 1858 and 1859 and who would be appointed Jewett's general assistant in October, 1865.

XI

Some Questions of Policy

THE CITY OF BOSTON had done well by the public library. It was housed in an impressive two-story building which, from Boylston Street, commanded a view northward over the Common lined on all sides by the fine, unostentatious houses of old Boston families. The building's brick façade was "made imposing by facings of massive brown stone," of which material the seven arches and the doorway were also fashioned. On the first floor there was an entrance hall that opened directly into a large room with a matted floor, plain seats and tables, and a long desk and counter for the library attendants. This, the room for circulation, was connected with a hall in the rear of the building having a gallery and twenty alcoves which contained the books most frequently demanded. Readers wishing to obtain books stepped to the circulation desk, asked one of the "lady clerks" for the register, entered their names, took a catalog and selected the books they desired; these were then procured by messengers. Also on the same floor were two other rooms, the one to the right of the circulation room a periodical room amply supplied with periodicals of the day, and that on the left a room reserved for the use of ladies. The two staircases in the entrance hall merged on a broad landing and, forming a broader flight, led readers up and into the middle of the very spacious second floor, or upper hall.

The upper hall was ninety-two feet long and thirty-eight feet wide. From its windows, set beneath a carved and fretted ceiling fifty-eight feet high, sunlight streamed down upon a black-and-white marble floor. Surrounding the wide, open space in the center of the hall were twenty Corinthian columns that rose to the ceiling. Between these, alcoves twenty feet deep and three floors in height bulged with books shelved on three sides. At the front of each alcove profane hands were kept back by a railing. The upper levels of the hall were reached by spiral flights of iron stairs, and, here too, the alcove pattern was repeated. In the central floor space of the hall were glass cases for exhibits, with gas lights overhead and tables and chairs for reading. Facing the head of the grand staircase stood the delivery desk, and, above it, a marble bust of Joshua Bates, for whom the hall was named after his death in 1864. The library building, which met fully Bates' specification "that the student on entering it will be impressed and elevated, and feel a pride that such a place is free to him," was regarded as one of the architectural ornaments of Boston.

Despite his absorption in the compilation of the index-catalogs, Jewett early gave some thought to encouraging the daily use of the library. Ever alert to the techniques and innovations of library service in Europe, he remarked with great interest the British and German experiences with branch library systems, especially the rapid increase in the number of readers and the soaring circulation figures at both main and branch libraries in Manchester, England. In 1859, he cautiously suggested to the trustees the establishment of branch libraries as a means of increasing "the popularity and usefulness" of the institution and servicing the rapidly-expanding Boston communities far distant from the Boylston Street area. But no action was forthcoming on so advanced a proposal. In 1867, the examining committee brought Jewett's suggestion once again to the attention of the trustees, yet no immediate steps were taken. Not until two years after Jewett's death would the doors of the first branch library open in East Boston.[1]

Almost from the beginning of its establishment the trustees and those interested in the progress of the library had been convinced of its worth and the good favor in which it was held by the public. They were, therefore, considerably concerned when, in 1860, it developed that there had been a decrease in the circulation of books between November 1859, and October 1860. The trustees assumed that this was the result of their having resolved in 1856 to purchase fewer and fewer "works of amusement" with each passing year, as well as of the opening in Boston of a number of circulating libraries able to provide these desired books of the hour. That the library's supply of current fiction was far behind the demand and that the circulating libraries springing up in the city were drawing upon the library clientele now seemed more than evident. Yet they believed they had acted wisely. The public library could not afford, financially, to compete with the circulating libraries, many of which purchased from fifty to one hundred copies each

[1] Its reading room alone was opened in the fall of 1870; its circulation for home use began in 1871.

of works enjoying great popularity, only to sell them at reduced prices after the demand had slackened. Moreover, the library had not been established to make available the multitudinous volumes of fiction that cascaded from the presses, especially those "not worth while to put into the hands of the young at public expense." Were it to acquire and circulate these, and abundant works of current nonfiction, solely for the purpose of increasing circulation figures, it would "be deprived of the means for fulfilling its higher and better purpose of furnishing works useful and instructive." That the library would constitute the keystone in the arch of public education had been an effective argument for its founding. How could they, then, reasonably request funds of the city council for achieving an end nowise similar or complementary?

Jewett, who explained the sudden decrease in circulation by pointing out that the "novelty of the enterprise" and the interest in the Boylston Street edifice had passed, also brushed aside all thought that the library should in any way seek to match the popularity of the circulating libraries. He further felt that any attempt to meet the demand for current fiction would thrust it "into a business competition with booksellers"—a probable consequence which his brother John, a publisher, may have brought to his attention.

In 1860, Ticknor, with great faith in the people and the possibility of winning them from "amusement" to "improvement" literature, instituted an experiment. He donated to the library ten to fifty copies each of several works, including the *Life of Amos Lawrence* by his son, and Everett's *Life of Washington*. The volumes were to be freely loaned, and he hoped that there would soon be a higher percentage of use "of books of this class" rather than those in "our collection of light literature." These "good and useful" books, when first placed upon the shelves were used and circulated, but scarcely a year had rolled around before the demand for them had fallen off. Indeed, by April, 1861, of 50 copies of Florence Nightingale's book on "healthy houses and good nursing," all but one were on the shelves; of 20 copies of Everett's *Washington*, 17 were in a similar state of repose, and all the copies of Lawrence's *Life* were gathering dust. The experiment was a dismal failure.

Although the library authorities refused to budge from their stand on current fiction, they made every effort to encourage suggestions from the public of other titles to be purchased. Article 9 of Chapter II of the By-Laws stated that

Whenever a book wanted by any one using the Library, does not belong to it, such person is particularly requested to enter the title of the book on a card furnished for the purpose, to which the person's name and residence shall be added.

Few persons availed themselves of this privilege. In 1860, after the decline in circulation, the trustees had printed notices put into every book lent for a fortnight requesting all readers who could not obtain a book they wanted *("except a novel")* because the book was not in the library or because there were insufficient copies to meet the demand, merely to write its title on a card "ready for the purpose." Several thousand notices were placed in the books lent during the period, yet less than twenty-five titles were asked for. The trustees, however, still kept an iron grip on the appropriations for fiction and light literature purchases. Their even-handed policy in supplying only a sufficient number of current popular volumes brought them diametrically opposed criticism from various quarters. In February 1861, several members of the city council began to scan the library budget, possibly with an eye to paring down its book funds. Jewett, in alarm, wrote Trustee William W. Greenough that he had been warned by a friend that a formal complaint would soon be lodged in the council against the abundance of popular books in the library, "and particularly of such works as Motley's." Apparently nothing came of this rumor. Contrariwise, by 1865 there was mounting dissatisfaction among the patrons of the library because the trustees were not purchasing a sizable number of the new books that were then available at the circulating libraries. So frequent and so strong were the grumbles that the examining committee of that year took occasion to bring the trustees up sharply, reminding them that "it is obviously the duty of the trustees to see that it be otherwise in the future, at least for the majority of books published." Yet, a more liberal policy in this respect was not pursued until the following administration.

In order to build up the library collections and supplement the Bates volumes, the books presented from time to time to the library, and the volumes purchased from available book funds (the 1858 book fund was $5,081; that of 1862 was $9,401), Jewett turned to the practice of exchanges. The passion for exchanges that had enabled him to lay so solid a foundation for the Smithsonian library in Washington found ample vent in Boston. Instead of employing the publications of the Institution as a basis for exchange—the practice of the Smithsonian—Jewett used the duplicate volumes in the library. As soon as the 1861 *Index* was off his shoulders he gave some attention to the problem. By 1863 he reported that arrangements had been made for disposing of the greater part of 5,237 items. Although lists of duplicates were prepared and sent frequently to institutions and libraries throughout the country, and although by 1864 "several hundred" volumes had been exchanged for "valuable works," it became more and more difficult to get rid of a large number of books in this manner. There were only a few libraries that did not already have the duplicate volumes on their shelves. The process of negotiation, of assigning to the donor's credit books of equal value with those he had presented to the library, and making the proper entries in the accessions catalog slowed down the process.

Many individuals who presented books to the library in this period realized the possibility of duplication and generally gave volumes with the understanding that their books might "be disposed of in any way most advantageous to the institution." In view of the difficulty of making exchanges, and the fact that if any of the books presented were sold the proceeds would have to be paid into the city treasury, Jewett in 1864 suggested that the trustees request permission from the city to sell, by private sale or auction, the books not needed by the library and to use the money obtained thereby for purchasing other books, which would then be credited to the account of the original donor. Within a year the trustees were granted the requisite authority, and the policy of selling duplicates was established. The exchange system with other libraries continued. Under Jewett's administration very heavy exchanges were made with the New York State Library, through the good offices and cooperation of S. B. Woodworth, its secretary. During the Civil War large quantities of duplicate books were distributed to the men from Boston in the armed forces and to military hospitals, and some were sent from time to time to the city hospital.

Of storms, minor and major, during Jewett's administration, none raged with more intensity than the Sunday-opening question. Well before 1859 a demand had arisen for opening the library to the public on the Lord's day. In that year the trustees, forced to consider the proposition, had deemed it "unnecessary and inexpedient." Yet the matter would not down. In 1864, 1865, and 1867 it rose again. In 1865 the mayor vetoed an order of the city council requesting the trustees to keep the reading room open on Sunday. That year the members of the examining committee so split during discussions of the subject that they decided not to reveal their views in their report and not to recommend any course to the trustees. When in 1867 the whole question came again to public attention, Jewett took to the field with shield and lance.

The controversy divided Bostonians as thoroughly as it had the examining committee of 1865. The cogent view of liberals was that the library should serve the mechanics, the laborers, and the general public who had no place open to them on Sunday for self-improvement. They did not think opening the library on Sunday any more of an "innovation," as opponents charged, than keeping open two thousand barrooms that did a rush business. They were outraged that the mayor and the trustees should keep the doors of the institution closed against the young men who were "thirsting after knowledge and not strong drink." They brushed aside as "very weak twaddle" the argument advanced from some quarters that to open the library would encourage mutilation and the theft of books, and noted with fiendish satisfaction that among the books missed from the Athenaeum *theological works* predominated! On the other hand, many ministers and men of true religious faith sincerely believed that the holiness of the Sabbath would be tarnished by attendance at the public library. If people sought the library on that day, what might happen to church attendance? If attendance declined, what would happen to morals? to religion? Why, open the library on Sunday and soon agitation would begin to throw open the doors of the theater! "Christians have yet to learn that Satan is in Boston and is not asleep," had thundered the *Christian Era* of May 18, 1865. In vain did a correspondent of the *Daily Evening Voice,* the official organ of the Workingmen's Assembly of Boston and vicinity, point out that most of those who would enter the walls of the library would be boys and men seeking the identical type of pleasure and education for which Bates, as a boy, had yearned. He also pointed out that the two strongest collections of the library had been given to it by Bowditch, a sailor boy, and Parker, a farmer boy who had

138

picked wild berries and sold them in the market in order to purchase his Latin grammar. The correspondent had no doubt that Bates, Bowditch, and Parker would have urged the Sunday opening. It was useless to tell him— as some persons had—that the trustees were best qualified to judge, for those august gentlemen were not known to "mix with or have any confidence in the 'plain people.'"

Matters reached a climax in 1867. During July the city council, under public pressure, held hearings on the question. Jewett testified at the third. He reiterated the various efforts of the trustees to arrive at a solution of the question, and put forth several reasons for their adverse decision on these occasions: no large public libraries were opened in England on Sunday; Edward Everett (who had died in 1865), while alive, had absolutely refused to hear the question discussed; the library employees were already overworked and additional labor on Sunday would only serve to bring many of them to the breaking point (some labored from nine in the morning to ten at night, with only a one and a quarter hour intermission for dinner); it was impractical to employ inexperienced persons to work one day in the library, and, should extra pay be given those willing to work, jealousy might rear her head among the staff; since the building had to be cleaned each day, extra custodial service would be necessary; influential patrons of the library, who held strong religious views, might be displeased and might withdraw their financial support.

Jewett's personal stand was reinforced by his deep religious convictions. A devoted member of Christ

Church, Quincy, he served for years as senior warden or as superintendent of the Sabbath school. Seldom was he absent from his family's side in their pew on Sundays, and on more than one occasion he rose from a sickbed to "worship the Lord." His feeling that the Sabbath ought to be passed in religious pursuits influenced his position on Sunday opening of the library. The accusation made by a witness at one of the council hearings, to the effect that he did not wish it open because he did not care to travel to Boston from his home in Braintree, was merely an ungracious and feeble thrust.

In any case, the city council, after pondering the evidence and casting an eye on the municipal coffers, declined to recommend a Sunday opening. The hubbub died away but the issue remained to plague Jewett's successor. After Jewett's death *Zion's Herald* would recall that "his opposition to the opening of the Library on the Lord's day was mainly the cause of the defeat of that anti-Christian design."

There were, for Jewett's consideration through the years, the usual problems centering around public relations and the conduct of the public within the walls of the institution. Borrowers who, irritated by slights in service, took pen in hand, had to have their feelings salved by reasoned letters. No one rose more quickly than Jewett to the defense of his staff against complaints he regarded as unjustified. It mattered not the source. In the fall of 1866, for instance, Trustee Henry I. Bowditch, the eminent physician, was informed by a lady, to whom he had given his personal card inscribed with a request that she be allowed to borrow a book, that she

140

had had to wait for half an hour for service and that, when all seemed in vain, she had departed in disgust. This situation, in which other readers might have found themselves, was *"wholly wrong,"* Bowditch wrote Jewett. And he asked the superintendent to see that the lady received the book she desired, trusting "that hereafter her valuable time will not be lost at the public library."[2] To this note Jewett drafted a firm, albeit courteous, reply.

9 Nov. 1866

My Dear Sir,—

No one at the Library, so far as I can ascertain, has any recollection of Miss Adam or of her errand here in June last. There is certainly misunderstanding somewhere.

Knowing as I do the character & habits of every attendant in this Library, it is to me as inconceivable that any one would treat with the slightest disrespect or inattention a person who came here & made known intelligibly such a request as that of Miss Adam, as it is that any one here would ever treat with neglect any recommendation you might give.

There is not a person in the Library, likely at any time to be at the desk, who would not immediately have told Miss Adam if she make known her errand that under the Rules she was entitled to use the Library. She is a teacher, it seems, in this city, & as such can receive cards whether she resides in the city or not, & whether she is recommended or not.

I cannot accuse myself or others of any wrong in this matter. Nor can I conceive that her want of success last June is due to any thing else but the failure of the attendant to comprehend what was sought for & this failure may have been owing to the misfortune of the one party in communi-

[2]Henry I. Bowditch to Jewett, dated "Thursday PM"; Letters and Documents Relating to the Administration of the Library, Boston Public Library.

cating, or of the other in understanding the communication. Your letter has I confess grieved me.

I remain

Yours faithfully[3]

Jewett could hardly have solved the recurring problem of keeping from the library those who sought its comforts for purposes other than reading. In addition to those seeking a quiet place for a nap, or shelter from inclement weather, the lovesick swain and his lady were to be found. It was a known fact that personal advertisements appeared in the public prints arranging trysts there, so known, indeed, that opponents of a Sunday opening had cited them in order to argue that the city council ought not to permit the library, which its promoters had intended as a place of moral uplift, to provide rendezvous "not always for innocent purposes." A member of the examining committee of 1865 reported that once, in Bates Hall, he himself had witnessed "a gentle *tête-a-tête* . . . being carried on by a young couple, who had found the luxurious chairs a pleasant spot in which to pass an agreeable hour." Other individuals had observed similar situations elsewhere. Not without reason did Dr. James Rush in his bequest of 1869 to the Philadelphia Library Company stipulate: "Let the library not keep cushioned seats for time-wasting and lounging readers."

Throughout his administration Jewett often found his time absorbed by questions pertinent to library economy in general. Though these subjects appear small and picayune to a later generation, they provided in their day material for many a heated discussion. On the problem

[3]C. C. Jewett to H. I. Bowditch, *ibid.*

142

of denoting the size of a book on the catalog card, for example, there was a difference of opinion and practice. Some employed the binder's signature—folio, quarto, octavo, duodecimo; others measured the first full signature page in inches and tenths. In his work on the construction of stereotype catalogs, Jewett had called attention to the need for a universal adoption of the latter, instructing the librarian thus:

The librarian should use a small square or rule, marked with inches and tenths. The first number given should represent the height, and the second, the breadth of the page. In the catalogue, the measurement would be recorded thus:—

$$8° \; (7.3 \times 4.2)$$

that is, fold of sheet, 8vo; measuring, 7 inches and 3 tenths in height, by 4 inches and 2 tenths in breadth.

Such an indication of size was necessary in catalogs, said he, because it distinguished between different editions of the same work and conveyed some idea of the size of the volume to one who had never seen it. By 1863, when William P. Tucker compiled the *Catalogue of the Library of Bowdoin College,* a compromise had been reached between the long-established "signature" size and Jewett's; the abbreviation commonly employed was given first, followed by the height of the book in inches and tenths.

The binding of pamphlets was another moot question on which Jewett had strong convictions. There were those who grouped several pamphlets by subject and had them bound in one volume and shelved amid their proper classification in the library. Jewett followed the practice of the British Museum, whereby pamphlets were separately cataloged and singly bound. He then had them shelved so as to form a distinct pamphlet collection.

Despite his numerous activities, Jewett, frequently importuned for advice from scholars and suggestions from librarians throughout the country, readily took up his pen. Thus to William Leonhard Gage:

9 March 1863

My Dear Sir,

I feel ashamed of my delay in writing to you, & can only say by way of apology, that I have been very busy, & what I had to say did not seem of immediate importance. But I ought at least to have thanked you for affording me the pleasure of perusing your Steffens[4] manuscript.[5] I read it through with great satisfaction. The selections seem to me to be made with excellent judgment & taste, & the style of the translation is remarkably easy & appropriate. I believe that the book will be a popular one. Its graphic, animated, & withal perfectly authentic, pictures of the celebrities of a wonderful period will surely be regarded with much interest by every one acquainted with the great names & great productions in German literature & science during the first half of this century.

I thought of suggesting to you to make extracts from the portion of Steffens' work relating to his early life & also from the part concerning the war of liberation [against Napoleon]. These would give the book more completeness as a biography & his military career is characteristic—some of it quite amusing & particularly interesting just at this time. But I suppose your aim was to give within the limits of a small book all that was most necessary to exhibit his activities and associations as a man of science & letters, & it was perhaps better thus

[4]Heinrich Steffens, 1773-1845.
[5]*The story of my career, as student at Freiberg and Jena, and as professor at Halle, Breslau and Berlin.*

144

to restrict yourself. Perhaps, too, you were influenced by the fact that copious extracts from the parts passed lightly over by you had been translated & published in London, by Murray in 1848, "Adventures on the road to Paris" &c. I have looked into this book since reading your manuscript & have found myself more pleased with it than I expected to be. The copy in our library bears marks of much use.

I regret that I cannot give you from my own recollections of Steffens something which would be of public interest. More than eighteen years have passed since I had the honor & advantage of a brief acquaintance with him. I cannot now refer to my notes written at the time & I remember little beyond the impression he made upon me, which was I think altogether like that one would receive by reading his autobiography as presented to English readers in your book.

It was in the latter part of the year 1844 that I became acquainted with him, I think through the family of Prof. Von Raumer.[6] I met him repeatedly; several times at his own house. On one occasion he placed me by his side at the table, that he might converse about America. I shall never forget the kindness of his manner, nor the warm interest he expressed in our country & its institutions. His conversation was full of vivacity. I was surprised & delighted at his rapid & highly poetical sketches of the scenery & physical features of a land he had never seen.

I remember at one time being with him when Jenny Lind was present. I think it was at the house of Tieck, the poet. It was her first winter in Berlin & she was received not only in public but in Society, so far as she would accept invitations, with the greatest enthusiasm. I allude to her to mention the patriotic pride with which Steffens spoke of her as a Northern European. His whole manner & expression was striking & beautiful, not to be soon forgotten.

[6]Friedrich Ludwig Georg von Raumer, 1781-1873.

145

It was during that winter he finished the tenth & last volume of his "Was ich erlebte." He referred to it with charming simplicity, & once spoke of his living to bring it up so near to the close of his life, in words which soon after recurred to my mind as almost prophetic. It was I think not more than two or three weeks afterwards that I received from him one of the last invitations to his hospitable house which he ever gave out. Before the evening for the visit he was attacked with the sickness which so soon proved fatal to him. I was absent from Berlin at the time of his death, but I heard much of the deep & widespread grief it occasioned. Schelling[7] pronounced his eulogium. A part of it is, I believe, prefixed to the "Nachgelassene Schriften" published in Berlin in 1846.

There is quite a full account of Steffens in the "Neuer Nekrolog der Deutschen" for 1845—with a complete list of his writings.

Did you mention to me that you have corresponded with Guizot[8] respecting your book? I did not see anything from him. He must have been well acquainted with Steffens in Steffens's best days.

I have written on thus at length—merely to show my interest in your undertaking. If I had been able to communicate anything beyond indistinct impressions, I should have written sooner. What I could say however seemed to me of value to you only as it confirms evidence, elsewhere abundant, relative to the appearance, manners, & character of Prof. Steffens, whom I believe all who knew him regard as one of the most attractive & amiable of the men of genius of his day. I shall hope soon to see your book in print & your translations from Ritter[9] also.

I feel personally grateful to you for thus bringing these two

[7]Friedrich Wilhelm Joseph von Schelling, 1775-1854.
[8]François Pierre Guillaume Guizot, 1787-1874.
[9]Karl Ritter, 1779-1859.

names to be better known & better appreciated in America.

I remain

Yours very Sincerely[10]

Letters poured in upon him soliciting his opinion on various aspects of library economy. When the librarian of the Portland (Maine) Athenaeum desired recommendations respecting the breadth of alcoves and the height of shelves, when President Samuel G. Brown of Hamilton College, in New York, sought comments on the construction plans for a new library, each turned to Jewett.

At no time, apparently, did Jewett, hard pressed by duties, concern himself with one of the chief objectives resolved upon during the 1853 Conference, namely, the formation of a permanent association of librarians. It had been expected that his influence in Washington would have had a salutary effect in realizing that end. But his departure from the Smithsonian Institution had taken the leader of the movement from the proposed scene of activity, and all had gone by the board since the other members of the planning committee had declined to take the initiative. Jewett had been much too burdened from 1854 to 1856 to give attention to the matter. Soon after, the panic of 1857 came upon the country; then he became firmly established in Boston as superintendent, with many problems to attend to, and, in 1861, the Civil War began. Although the idea of a permanent library association doubtless continued to appeal to him and to others, its realization was to await till 1876 the magical touch of Melvil Dewey.

[10]Miscellaneous Manuscript Papers, Houghton Library, Harvard University.

XII

Some Problems of Administration

A MATTER of grave concern to Jewett, the trustees, and the various examining committees, was the mutilation of books. During the first years of the library there were occasional mutilations, such as markings and drawings in the margins of books, and the strewing therein of comments on particular passages, "to the disgust of all future readers." Such "ill-bred practices," Jewett felt, deserved the strongest reprehension and their perpetrators unsparing punishment. During the Civil War years the mutilation of books mounted to such an extent that by 1865 the examining committee demanded that vigorous measures be taken by the library authorities. On their annual tour of inspection they noted with great indignation that the desecration of library property was on the increase. They were shocked to find abuses too numerous to relate, although they cited as an example a "gross attack" on Abraham Lincoln "written in doggerel lines and surmounted by the late, so-called, Confederate States' flag" on the flyleaf of a "valuable work." The committee suggested that a better system of recording loans be devised, to prevent not only the "abuse" of books, but their loss as well.

Many volumes, indeed, were rapidly disappearing from the shelves of the library. So heavy had been the assaults on the lower hall collection that its index-catalogs had been "rendered imperfect" both by a loss of books and by the necessity of withdrawing from circulation those that were damaged and bescribbled. The trustees themselves lamented that in the reading room, alone, with its fine collection of periodical literature and reference works, abuses had become very serious:

Since the first of December last, [1864] forty-six numbers of different valuable journals have been stolen;—many more have been mutilated by cutting out what was deemed useful or agreeable by the persons who so shamelessly abused the privileges they enjoyed;—and a still greater number has been so wilfully defaced that it is necessary to replace them by other copies.

This sad situation was by no means confined to the lower hall. No one was more disturbed about it than Jewett. When he met the examining committee, before the upper hall was first thrown open to the public, he had remarked that the occasion was one of peculiar interest, for never again would all the books in that collection be found within its walls. When asked whether he did not propose to make an annual examination, he said that there would be no necessity for "such a ceremony, if the library were properly administered." Withal the time-honored "ceremony" had continued there as in the lower hall.

In 1866, at the prompting of the library and city authorities, the State Legislature passed a law providing severe penalties for the mutilation and defacement of library property, and this law, together with a new circulation system, reduced the abuse and loss of books.

Jewett, as soon as the suggestion of the examining committee of 1865 had been approved by the trustees, began to work upon a new system of recording loans. From the early days of the library loans had been recorded by jotting down the shelf and "order" number of each volume in a ledger. Neither the title of the book, the date due, nor the date when issued was noted therein. Irregularities were thus difficult to check. It was almost impossible to tell which books were overdue and who had them, until they had been returned by the borrower. Reliable information could not be obtained on "what class of books were most used, or how frequently such and such a book had been called for." Yet the ledger system continued to hold its own, unchallenged, in the libraries of the country "until the early days of the Civil War." In 1861, prior to the opening of the upper hall, Jewett had submitted a twenty-page report to the trustees (*Plan for the Circulation and Use of the Books in the Upper Hall of the Public Library*) in which he proposed that all holders of lower hall cards be allowed to use the upper hall, on issuance of a special card, this card to be left in the library. The date of issue of a book was to be stamped on a ticket attached to the cover of the book. Each borrower was to be given a blank form having a coupon, or stub, for the book he withdrew. On returning it he was to collect the coupon, and the other part of the receipt was then to be filed for the sake of the record. This adumbration of the modern charging system was an original idea with Jewett but, says Henry J. Carr, "it does not seem to have been put into use or, at least, not in its full form."

By 1866 Jewett had ready for the approval of the trustees a plan for recording loans by means of slips. His scheme called for the use of printed slips of paper, of uniform size, for each book to be charged out from the library. On each slip the library attendant would write a word or two of the title, the shelf and "order" number of the book, and the name and address of the borrower. He would then stamp the date of loan, on the slip, on the inside cover of the book, and on the borrower's card. The slip would be filed by shelf number, under the issue date. When the volume was returned, the slip and the borrower's card would be stamped, in a different colored ink, with the discharge date.

The slip system was swiftly initiated and as quickly proved its value. A larger number of books could be given out each day. Whereas under the ledger system only two persons could receive and charge books at a time without interfering with one another, under the slip system as many persons as could stand at the delivery desk might receive or return books, while as many as could be accommodated with stamps and table room could be engaged in charging them, "at one and the same time." All told, there was greater ease, quietness, and regularity of service, with a minimum of conference among the library assistants. During the first three months the system was in operation, Jewett observed with much pride that no imperfections developed. As soon as experience established its merits, other libraries throughout the country hastened to adopt it. By the close of the century it had become the main system for the circulation of books in a majority of American public libraries.

The circulation of books from the lower hall had always been too slow for borrowers, who frequently complained of the service there. No sooner had he formulated the slip system than Jewett, with his usual ingenuity, sought to devise a means of speeding up the circulation process and reducing the borrower's waiting time. With H. R. Taylor, a cabinetmaker, he designed a mechanical indicator frame which would show, without the aid of a library attendant, whether a book desired by a reader was in its place on the shelf or out on loan. The "indicator" was thus described by Horace G. Wadlin:

In an upright framework strips of wood, each representing a shelf, were placed one above another. Reversible pins, each representing a book, were inserted in these strips. The strips carried the shelf numbers and the pins the book numbers, printed in black and white. When the book was lent, the pin was at once reversed, indicating the fact.

Merely by glancing at it a borrower could perceive whether a book he wished to send for was available. Although somewhat crude, this ingenious device served its purpose well, and not until 1875 did the library give up its use.[1]

Jewett's efforts to improve service to readers did not cause him to lose touch with the cataloging or acquisition of books. Under his administration the card system of cataloging became well known, although the initial impetus for the use of cards had come from Folsom at the

[1]Although this instrument of Jewett's invention was regarded as a novelty, it was subsequently discovered that the Manchester (England) Public Library had installed one similar in purpose about 1863.

Boston Athenaeum. The (official) card catalog, the accessions catalog, the shelf list, and the indexes to the catalogs of the lower and Bates Hall collections were the principal guides to the library holdings. The card catalog was in manuscript and contained authors, subjects, and titles filed in one alphabet. Titles were entered in full under the names of authors, with cross references from the names of subjects treated and important catchwords of the titles. Contents of collections were carefully set forth, with each article of the contents entered separately on a card filed under the author's name. Bibliographical notes were often added to the author cards. This catalog was connected, by a system of numbering, with other records of the library (accessions catalog, shelf lists, and fund-books), so that these could be easily referred to for additional information.

In 1864, Jewett, in his annual report, called attention to the fact that it had been necessary thus far to print six supplementary lists to the *Index* to the lower hall and one supplement to that of the upper hall. He deemed it important now to consolidate the *Index* and the supplements to the lower hall. He suggested that either the supplements be combined and cross references added, so as to form a single large supplemental volume, or that the *Index* and supplements be reprinted in one alphabet. What he looked forward to was the printing of the index-catalogs of both halls in one alphabet, with short titles under authors and subjects. By 1866 nothing had been done in that direction, probably because of the expense which would have been involved and the awkward size of the volume Jewett contemplated. That year the examining committee, of which Ticknor was chairman, proposed that a monthly bulletin of current acquisitions be printed. This publication, it was hoped, would enable the library to dispense with annual supplements to the index-catalogs, would inform the public more expeditiously of the titles acquired, and would become a means of spreading information "respecting the library, its progress, and its various wants." So sage and feasible a suggestion was instantly acted upon. The following year (October) the first number of the *Bulletin* made its appearance, thereafter to be issued at intervals for sale at two cents a copy.

During Jewett's years in office the perennial problem of increasing library salaries came to the fore. When appointed superintendent he had been granted an annual salary of $2,000. This was at that time a princely sum. The highest yearly salary of a librarian in a public institution was $1,900, paid to the head of the State Library of Massachusetts. The Mercantile Library in New York was then offering $1,500 and Harvard College $1,300 a year. From 1858 to 1866 Jewett's salary merely inched forward, and by the latter year the increased cost of living had put a severe financial strain upon him.

In 1866 intrigue was afoot. While the committee on salaries of the city council was laboring over its annual report, Librarian Edward Capen, it appears, kept himself well posted on their proceedings, and, without having consulted the trustees, sent the municipal body a private letter, of telling effect, and had his salary raised to $2,000, a sum not too far from Jewett's. When the committee's printed report appeared and Jewett realized what had transpired, his indignation was understandably and rightfully extreme. It was only by a strong exercise of the self-control he had attained since his Washington days that he curbed his emotions. With considerable justice he chided amiable Trustee William W. Greenough. He had hoped, he said, that the trustees would of their own volition have recommended an increase in his salary, but now, since no representation had been made to the committee that it was unsatisfactory, it was to remain the same. Somewhat sadly he wrote:

. . . It seems to have been supposed that I am quite independent of salary. But the last few years which have brought wealth to so many have deprived me of nearly all I had to rely upon, and I get nothing from my wife's property till the estate is divided.

I have made great sacrifices for the library. The best years of my life have been given to it without adequate compensation. I have acted unselfishly. I have sought the interests of the Library primarily, my own remotely. I have no love of money—no desire for stylish living—but I do feel that I am entitled to a respectable livelihood, such as I have always been accustomed to. For the last two years or more, I have received what would have been less than a thousand dollars a year when I took this office. . . .[2]

Sympathetic Mr. Greenough suggested a course Jewett might pursue, but the superintendent refused to consider it because he believed that any movement for a higher salary must come from the trustees and not from himself. Said he:

[2]To William W. Greenough, March 29, 1866, Letters and Documents Relating to the Administration of the Library, Boston Public Library.

. . . I cannot resist the conviction that any movement in which I should take the initiative before any Committee of the City Government for my benefit, would end in further disappointment & mortification. It would wear to them the appearance of an appeal against, or at least beyond the judgment of the Trustees. It would so appear to myself & I could not therefore have the heart to make it. . . .[3]

Sorrowfully, he noted that his salary in no way measured up to that of the "masters" of the public schools: the High School, the Latin School, and the Girls' High and Normal Schools. Yet his responsibilities were as great and his work commensurate with theirs. He might well have emphasized also that among the more telling arguments offered for the founding of the public library had been its potentiality as an adjunct to the public schools, whose very principals now earned more than he. Moreover, had not the trustees themselves said, in the memorial of 1857, that the work of a "Librarian in a great public library nearly resembles that of a professor in a seminary of learning"? Had not the examining committee of 1865 stated that the office of superintendent was "on a par with that of the Presidency of a University"?

In the midst of this mourning Jewett probably did not forget that two years earlier he had greatly antagonized the city council in an untoward manner by a frank avowal of his political beliefs.

Jewett was a member of the Democratic Party. His outlook in matters national, sectional, and local was conservative. In Rhode Island he had been a witness to Dorr's Rebellion and in a pamphlet published anony-

[3]March 31, 1866; *ibid.*

mously, *Close of the Late Rebellion in Rhode Island: an Extract from a Letter by a Massachusetts Man Resident in Providence* (1842), had excoriated Dorr and his followers. Dorr, "cold, calculating, supremely selfish and doggedly obstinate," he characterized as a mere demagog; the rebellion as a sinister subterfuge. While the "ostensible object of the movement" was the extension of the suffrage, he wrote, the real object was to bring a few broken-down political outcasts into power. His opinions coincided with those of the faculty of Brown University, who, like true Rhode Island Democrats and many old Whigs, were anti-Dorrites.

In Washington, before Smithsonian troubles began to brew, Jewett's conservative, Democratic social sense was offended by the announcement that Senator Hannegan, "an ignorant, dissipated Irishman" had been named minister to Berlin by President Polk. Bewailing the ignorance of the Northern and Southern Whigs who backed the appointment, Jewett had pleaded with Folsom to suggest George P. Marsh's appointment to Jared Sparks and Edward Everett, and then to urge both men to write John M. Clayton, the Secretary of State, suggesting Marsh for Hannegan's post. It was to no avail. Hannegan received the appointment and journeyed to Berlin, where his love of the bottle shortly caused a scandal and necessitated his recall.

Jewett, unlike his brother John, apparently took no active part in the anti-slavery movement. Whether he had sympathy for that cause is not quite certain. He dreaded the thought of secession by the Southern states. After the presidential election of 1856, he praised the choice of James Buchanan, observing with considerable relief that "Mr. Buchanan is a prudent & cautious man; if not baited by disunion hounds till he loses his reason, he will not put in peril our prosperity."[4]

It was in 1864 that Jewett had run afoul of the Boston authorities who held the library purse strings. At the time General George B. McClellan visited the city, seeking "to influence the canvass against the nomination of President Lincoln for a second term."[5]

Since the beginning of the Civil War Lincoln had sought to bind Republicans and Democrats to the war effort and, early in his administration, had given military positions to members of both parties. Upon the exit of Republican Simon Cameron from the cabinet, he had brought in Edwin M. Stanton, a Democrat, as Secretary of War. Most Democrats, however, remained in their own party. By 1864 there was much opposition to Lincoln's prosecution of the war, and the Peace Democrats began to clamor for an end to the conflict and a restoration of the Union; and they turned to McClellan as a candidate likely to defeat Old Abe. In Boston, unlike New York and other cities in loyal states, Republican sympathies were in the ascendancy by election time. Jewett, either not divining that fact, or better, not caring to compromise his political principles, was most outspoken about his views. His utterances fell harshly upon the ears of the city councilmen, and once the campaign fever had subsided they turned their attention to Jewett. Under the

[4]Jewett to an unidentified person, January 9, 185[7], *ibid.*
[5]Edward Capen to Justin Winsor, January 27, 1882, Winsor Papers, Massachusetts Historical Society.

ordinance in effect, the trustees had the power annually to nominate their choice for superintendent, but his election and salary were to be determined by the city council. So thoroughly had Jewett displeased its members that he almost lost his re-election. When he learned of the marginal vote that had saved him he announced his determination to resign, unless he would not again be subjected to an election by the council, for he did not choose to trim his sails to political winds. These tidings reached the public prints. On June 2, 1865, the *Congregationalist* commented:

We are sorry to hear that Mr. Jewett has resigned the charge of the noble institution; and from what we hear, we fear that his withdrawal is peremptory.

Jewett's decision was not peremptory. The trustees, employing their persuasive powers upon him, hastened at the same time to bring pressure on the council to amend the 1858 ordinance so that their board might have the authority to appoint the superintendent "with permanent tenure, subject to removal by the council for cause," and to fix his salary; while the examining committee of that year took occasion to remark that the office of superintendent "should be removed far above even the mere breath of political partisanship," and wisely added that no man would long "submit to the annual uncertainties of political strife in a matter of his election." In 1865 an ordinance was passed permitting the trustees to appoint the superintendent, whose salary, however, was to be determined by the council. Jewett's anxieties were somewhat relieved, but the real core of the principle at issue passed over to the Justin Winsor administration. It took Winsor's dramatic resignation in 1877 to bring the matter to a head and force a final solution.

XIII

After a Decade of Superintendency,
The End

ON NEW YEAR'S DAY, 1868, Jewett looked back upon ten
years of administering the affairs of the Boston Public
Library. A sense of satisfaction could scarcely have escaped him. Against 70,851 volumes in 1858, the library
now possessed some 140,000. Its resources had been
especially enriched during that period by the receipt of
several outstanding collections. In 1858, the sons of
Nathaniel Bowditch, famed nautical mathematician, presented their father's library of 2,500 volumes, together
with 29 volumes of his personal manuscripts. In 1855,
through the efforts of Joseph Story, a former president
of the Common Council, and James Buchanan, then
minister to Great Britain, the Commissioners of the Royal
Patent Office offered to donate a set of a work then in
course of publication, which contained the specifica-
tions for all the patents taken out in England from the
year 1617. This generous offer the trustees warmly wel-
comed, for no work was "so replete with practical instruction to the machinist, the artisan, the inventor and
every person connected with the great industrial interests
of the community." By 1858 the volumes had begun to
arrive and thus was the foundation of the Patent Collection laid. In 1860, under the provisions of his will, the
library of Theodore Parker, minister-reformer, containing

11,061 volumes, was received; not until 1881, upon the death of Mrs. Parker, who had retained a few favorite books, were the remaining valuable volumes deposited. The collection was rich in grammars and dictionaries of many foreign languages and dialects, and in works of importance in history, jurisprudence, theology, and the classics—among them the one hundred volumes of Migne's *Patrologia*. The library of the Reverend Thomas Prince, who began its collection when he enrolled at Harvard College in 1703 and who bequeathed it to the Old South Church, was placed in the custody of the public library in 1866; it abounded in the rare books that Prince had employed in writing his history of New England.

When that perpetual criterion of supposed library vitality, the circulation statistics, had been completed, nothing was more calculated to impress the country at large, with its emerging public libraries, than the avid use the citizens of Boston made of their institution. Circulation had risen, from 149,468 volumes in 1859 to 208,963 eight years later. The library had become firmly established as a factor in popular education "and in this respect was without peer in the country." Jewett's index-catalogs had thrown open its resources to an intelligent and eager public, and his slip system and "indicator" had speeded their issue. The collections of the library had been freely and generously placed at the disposal of student and scholar alike. The deficiences of American libraries, on which George Livermore had thrown clear light in the *North American Review* in 1850, had received remedial treatment, and some credit was due to Jewett.

Scholars, appreciative of his efforts, rewarded him with membership in several societies, among them the American Association for the Advancement of Science, the New England Historic Genealogical Society, the American Antiquarian Society, and Phi Beta Kappa.

Boston in 1868 was still what it had been in 1850, the most favored section of America in the matter of libraries. It could boast of its book resources with justifiable pride, as its newspapers frequently did. Within its confines were the Athenaeum with 100,000 volumes, the state library with 28,500, the Mercantile Library with 20,000, the Boston Library with 19,000, the Massachusetts Historical Society with 18,500 and the Natural History Society with 12,000. Leading these institutions was the public library, some 140,000 volumes strong. Its growth seemed phenomenal when citizens recalled that it had received a solid foundation only fourteen years earlier. The dispatch and distinctiveness which Jewett had brought to its development had raised its impressive holdings above all the other libraries of Boston, Massachusetts, and New England. By 1868 the Boston Public Library stood second on the list of American libraries. It led the Astor Library with its 138,000 volumes; it was, in turn, led by the Library of Congress with 175,000. Yet, even here, there was need for a bit of qualification. The Congressional library increased its collection immensely, because, under the generous provisions of the copyright act, it received without cost a copy of every American book, because it received annual Congressional grants of $10,000 for the purchase of foreign books, and because it had no binding expense, as all such work was cared for at the "Government bindery." It had on deposit the library of the Smithsonian Institution and, in 1867, had acquired the vast Peter Force collection. The Boston Public Library had, perforce, to rely upon the appropriations of the city council and on the bibliothecal and financial gifts of its citizens and benefactors. To be sure, the city council had been generous in its appropriations, and, under Jewett's administration, the budget had risen from $19,890 (1858) to $52,658 (1867). A consideration of these factors rendered the library's progress all the more phenomenal. Small wonder that the City of Boston, the trustees, and the users of the library were pleased with the progress of the institution and the conduct of its affairs by the Superintendent.

To state with definiteness and precision the degree to which Jewett's leadership, or that of Everett, or Ticknor, or the Board of Trustees, was responsible for the development of the library in this period is a difficult task. Jewett was responsible to the trustees for the administration of the library and of a staff of more than thirty-five individuals. His authority was limited to the extent that he was not sole policy maker. His decisions had to be taken under advisement by the Board of Trustees and had to meet with their approval. In 1863—a typical year —the board was headed by Edward Everett. The other members were George Ticknor, John P. Bigelow, Nathaniel B. Shurtleff, William W. Greenough, John S. Tyler and Henry A. Drake. Both Everett and Ticknor were strong personalities and to a considerable degree they dominated the early boards. Whether they dominated the Superintendent is to be questioned.

That there may have been some serious clashes of opinion between Everett, Ticknor and Jewett does not appear to be an unwarranted assumption, for all three were men of determination and firm will. Jewett was a man who could hold his own, and it is not likely that he was always bested in their occasional verbal encounters. He was certainly assertive when circumstance demanded; he carried the day in maintaining his elaborate cataloging practices, despite what appears to have been the opposition of Ticknor. As he lagged behind the board in proposing reforms along certain lines, such as a much needed reorganization of the administrative setup and the cataloging department, so he sometimes marched ahead of them in suggesting, for example, the establishment of branch libraries. More often, however, his views on problems like Sunday opening, and supplying the public with fiction and copies of books in current demand, appear to have coincided with those of the trustees.

While he was superintendent, Jewett posed for a photograph—the only likeness of the mature librarian that has been reproduced in publications through the years. Some features—the full dark face, dark hair, aquiline nose, bushy whiskers, even the small mouth with its somewhat sensuous lips—taken as a whole, instantly convey the impression of firmness and authority, tinged with a slight amount of austerity. The recessed grey eyes, on the other hand, seem kind and gentle, and appear to look with sympathy and understanding upon a world whose sorrows and sufferings are made bearable through God's mercy and love. The photograph to an extent denotes on the one hand a highly sensitive intellectual whose calling forced administrative work upon him, and a man gifted with the art of inspiring others to work and cooperate with him by his gentleness of manner. On the other hand, it suggests a man who could meet with his equals, exert initiative whenever he felt it necessary to do so, stand his ground when he thought he was in the right, and who, ever conscious of his prerogatives, could fly into a rage when crossed by those he believed were employing underhanded and unmanly methods for the achievement of their ends.

If Jewett's library achievements—which undoubtedly gave him a sense of victory over his Washington enemies and restored his self-confidence—were rewarding, they hardly equaled his domestic bliss. Ever a family man, he derived the greatest joy and delight from watching with his wife over their three children. (Their second daughter, Eleanor Punchard, had been born May 31, 1867.) A devout Christian, he faithfully lived up to his religious duties and gave much time to church affairs. He did not neglect the obligations of social life and could be found at distinguished gatherings where, as at the home of Richard Henry Dana (senior), he passed pleasant evenings in company with Justin Winsor, Oliver Wendell Holmes, and other men of letters.

As the second decade of his superintendency opened, Jewett had on his agenda many projects, including a catalog of the Prince library. But he was not to see their completion. Although enjoying apparent full health, the early years of struggle and nervous exhaustion in Washington, the failure of his cherished Smithsonian projects, the heavy responsibilities entailed in executing his father-in-law's estate, his efforts to care for a growing family—all coupled with his exacting library labors—had been silently claiming their toll upon his much overworked system.

On January 8, 1868, a little past three o'clock, he was writing at his desk in the library. Suddenly his hand grew numb. Within a few moments the sensation had spread until it had reached his head and induced a state of partial paralysis. Mr. Ford, the janitor, who was in the office during the attack of apoplexy, helped him to a couch and speedily procured medical attention. After lying down for a few hours the smitten man begged to be taken to his family. He was helped to a carriage, but on the way to Braintree and his beloved ones Jewett lapsed into a state of unconsciousness from which he never emerged, and, at about one o'clock in the morning, passed away. To the last, faithful Mr. Ford remained by his side. The funeral services, held at Trinity Church, Boston, on January 11, were attended by members of the family, the trustees and attendants of the Boston Public Library, fellow librarians, scholars, and "many men of prominent station and name." At the conclusion of the service his remains were deposited in a vault beneath the church.

XIV

Conclusions

BEFORE SUMMARIZING Jewett's contributions to librarianship in America it ought to be noted that he lived in an age when the individual librarian, working largely alone and unaware of what had been done or was being done elsewhere, struck out for himself in attempting to solve the many problems that came his way. Advice from a small number of colleagues who might also be friends, an acquaintance with their limited experience, or some slight knowledge of European methods, were the best that could be hoped for, and even these opportunities and advantages were enjoyed by a very few men, among them Jewett and Cogswell. It was a period when the growth and development of libraries began to compel changes in policies and procedures that had been long established, when adaptation and modification of old techniques did not always suffice and the invention of new ones became necessary, when the mounting use of rapidly increasing library collections dictated the fashioning of more serviceable and elaborate keys to unlock the secrets of accumulating treasures. These were the days when the British Museum had only a manuscript author catalog to guide its readers; when the student at Harvard College went to a card catalog, stood the card for the particular book he desired on end, and rang a bell on top of the catalog case that summoned the page who memorized the shelf number of the volume and hastened to fetch it. The librarians of the time found themselves constantly confronted with manifold and perplexing situations. How ought loans to be recorded so as to provide much-needed information for analyses of service and reading interests, to accommodate readers, and to speed up the circulation of books? Should the catalogs of fast-growing collections be printed, when, even before the last page had passed through the press, they would be out of date? If so, what type of catalog, author or classed, should be compiled? What forms of entry employed? Were pamphlets to be bound singly or in groups? To the solution of these and other problems Charles Coffin Jewett ardently and unselfishly devoted himself. His achievements were substantial and constitute an impressive array of positive contributions to librarianship in the period 1841-1868.

While at Brown University he stimulated the use of the library, brought fame to it and to himself by his 1843 *Catalogue,* and increased the value of its collection by his judicious purchases in Europe. He gained a first-hand knowledge of Continental and English library economy that he later put to good use, and he undoubtedly did much to raise librarianship in the estimation of his contemporaries by combining scholarship with bibliography. At Washington he established and gave direction to the Smithsonian Institution library, which he built up in six years from several scattered volumes held by a few officials to a collection of more than thirty-two thousand volumes. Here he launched various projects and, save for the heartbreaking failure of the stereotyping scheme, succeeded in carrying a large number of them to completion. The acceptance by Congress of his recommendations on the transmission of copyright application copies of books free of postage; his survey of the library resources of the United States which, revised by another, remained an unrivaled source of information until the appearance of the famed 1876 report of the United States Bureau of Education; and his efforts to insure the success of the 1853 convention and his role there in focusing public attention on the activities of librarians were all noteworthy accomplishments. At the Boston Public Library he engaged in his more substantial labors: the monumental dictionary index-catalogs, then the *ne plus ultra* in cataloging; the well-developed exchange system; the recording of the circulation of books on separate slips, rather than in a ledger; and the invention of the "indicator." Under his administration the system of cataloging on cards was carried to a high point; the salary and book budgets of the library were increased; valuable collections, such as the library of Theodore Parker, were left to the institution because of faith in the conduct of its affairs; the circulation of books, which were made freer of access than was common in that day, rose by leaps and bounds. And the cause of the profession was advanced by his constant communication with European librarians and his eagerness to inform himself about their ways of doing things.

When Jewett died in 1868 the mushrooming of public libraries in the United States was in the offing, the library profession as such unrecognized, and cooperation among its practitioners a desire yet to be satisfied. No national association of librarians and no periodical devoted entirely to their interests existed. Of uniform procedure there was pitifully little, of standardized equipment none. Still, it was during his lifetime that many a fertile acre of the field of librarianship was tilled and seeded and much that grew from bud to blossom in later years was planted.

Today, more than a century after Jewett entered his illustrious career, the library profession is benefiting from his labors and his ideas. The Library of Congress card is the answer to the problem he sought to solve by his plan for centralized cataloging at the Smithsonian. The principle that prompted the initial distribution of Library of Congress cards is, to a considerable degree, that that inspired Jewett's scheme—the inexpensive production by one agency of uniform registration of titles. When he drew up his outline he did not divine the tremendous growth of libraries or the extensive use of cards for cataloging. Had he lived longer, to see these, it is highly possible that he might have suggested the printing of cards by a central agency for distribution to libraries along the lines he laid out in the stereotyping plan. In any case, the principle of centralized, or cooperative cataloging is his. Likewise, the idea of a union catalog in the nation's capital. Today the union catalog in Washington, where the location of more than ten million titles of works not duplicated in the Congressional library may be found, has fully lived up to Jewett's prediction that it would be an invaluable bibliographical apparatus and of service in stimulating interlibrary loans. Jewett's argument that separate plates of individual titles might be arranged to print any type of catalog, bibliography, or index may be said to have furnished one of the principles on which the cumulative productions of the H. W. Wilson Company are based.

It was Jewett who established the dictionary arrangement of catalogs that has endured to this day, and who compiled the rules for cataloging that not only influenced Cogswell in his work on the Astor Library catalogs, and the labors of others, but provided a basis for the 1876 code of Charles Ammi Cutter which, in turn, aided in the formulation of later rules. It was Jewett who broke the hold of the ledger system of recording loans by inaugurating the slip system, which, with modifications, still survives.

He was one of the first librarians in America to propose the instituting of branch libraries, to survey the library resources of the land from primary materials, and to draft and employ principles of accurate bibliographical transcription, thus paving the way for the rise of scientific bibliography in America and placing Sabin, Evans, Eames and others of that noble calling under obligation. And he was one of the first to advocate cooperation among librarians, and to look forward to the formation of a permanent national association of l_rarians.

Much honor, therefore, is due the efforts of this great originator and bold innovator in whom Nature chose to mingle, as is her wont, traits that often appeared incompatible: boundless energy, sympathetic understanding of human problems, enthusiasm, egotism, resentfulness of affronts, assertiveness, piety, kindliness, and a certain quickness of temper. Concerning the exertions of librarians he once wrote:

. . . our pursuits are not of such a nature, as to reward our labors by brilliant discourses, or results that will resound in the busy world. We must work hard and long, with small visible effect, and in the track where hundreds, more learned than ourselves perhaps, have worked before us. . . .[1]

While he himself worked to good effect in old tracks, his greatest success and satisfaction came in the blazing of new paths. Although, since the close of the nineteenth century, the luster of his achievements has perhaps grown somewhat dim, now, at the midpoint of the twentieth century Jewett stands in the position he will continue to occupy in American library history—an assured and eminent one.

[1]Jewett to Seth Hastings Grant, August 16, 1853, in George B. Utley, "The Librarians' Conference of 1853" (unpublished ms.) p. 42.

Selected Bibliographical Notes

Time has dealt harshly with the manuscript letters of Jewett. To date, no considerable body of personal papers has come to light. There are a few letters in the Archives Collection at Brown University; none at the Smithsonian Institution, where the fire of 1865 destroyed the official records; some at the Boston Public Library, both in the official correspondence and in the Charles Folsom Papers. Other Jewett letters are found in the correspondence files of the American Antiquarian Society, in the Charles Sumner Papers and the miscellaneous manuscript papers at the Harvard University Library, in the Library of Congress Papers in the Manuscript Division of that institution, in the Seth Hastings Grant Papers, and in the miscellaneous manuscript papers at the New York Public Library. These have been drawn upon, as have the Jewett family papers in the possession of Amos E. Jewett, the Justin Winsor Papers in the possession of Miss Penelope B. Noyes and the Massachusetts Historical Society, and the Herbert Baxter Adams Papers at the Johns Hopkins University Library.

Among biographical articles on Jewett the most useful and informative are by William B. Trask in the *New England Historical and Genealogical Register* 22:365-66 (1868), by William C. Lane in the *Dictionary of Ameri-*

can *Biography* 10:66 (New York, 1933), and by Reuben A. Guild in the *Library Journal* 12:507-11 (1887). The latter, entitled "Memorial Sketch of Prof. Charles C. Jewett," and written by a good friend, is an admirable survey of Jewett's activities but gives the least attention to his Boston Public Library years. It is a revised and enlarged version of a "Biographical Notice of Charles Coffin Jewett" which Guild wrote for the *Providence Evening Press* of January 10, 1868, and which was several times reprinted in that city and later by the Smithsonian Institution.

CHAPTER I

Jewett genealogy is found in *Vital Records of Salem*, volumes 2 and 5 (Salem, 1918); Frederick C. Jewett, *The History and Genealogy of the Jewetts of America* (New York, 1908) 2 vols.; H. L. Jewett, "Some Additions to the Published History of the Jewett Family," *The Grafton Magazine of History and Genealogy* 2:199-209 (1910); George B. Blodgett, comp., *Early Settlers of Rowley, Massachusetts*, rev. and ed. by Amos E. Jewett (Rowley, 1933); Amos and E. M. A. Jewett, *Rowley, Massachusetts* (Rowley, 1946). Jonathan Greenleaf, *Sketches of the Ecclesiastical History of the State of Maine* (Portsmouth, 1821), has information on Paul Jewett, as does Guild, "Memorial Sketch" *(supra)* which this chapter follows in outline. Of value is H. K. Rowe, *History of Andover Theological Seminary*. Brown University and the library during Jewett's days as student, librarian, and professor of modern languages are treated in Reuben A. Guild, *History of Brown University, with*

Illustrative Documents (Providence, 1867); R. A. Guild, "The College Library," *Library Journal* 10:216-21 (1885); Francis and H. L. Wayland, *A Memoir of the Life and Labors of Francis Wayland* (New York, 1867) 2 vols.; Robert P. Brown, ed., *Memories of Brown; Traditions and Recollections Gathered from Many Sources* (Providence, 1909); Walter C. Bronson, *The History of Brown University, 1764-1914* (Providence, 1914). Conditions in college libraries are described in W. N. C. Carlton, "College Libraries in the Mid-nineteenth Century," *Library Journal* 32:479-86 (1907). Jewett's 1843 catalog is favorably commented upon, among other places, in the *North American Review* 58:227-36 (1844) and *Christian Era* 8:499 (1844). Professor Jewett is mentioned in James B. Angell, *The Reminiscences of James Burrill Angell* (New York, 1920), and his physical description is given on his 1843 passport in the files of the United States Department of State.

CHAPTER II

On the establishment and history of the Smithsonian Institution the following are indispensable: Smithsonian Institution, *The Smithsonian Institution: Journals of the Board of Regents, Reports of Committees, Statistics* (Washington, 1879); William J. Rhees, comp. and ed., *The Smithsonian Institution: Documents Relating to its Origin and History, 1835-1899* (Washington, 1901) 2 vols.; George B. Goode, ed., *The Smithsonian Institution, 1846-1896: the History of the First Half Century* (Washington, 1897); Paul H. Oehser, *Sons of Science; The Story of the Smithsonian Institution and its Leaders*

(New York, 1949). A useful account is W. P. True, *The First Hundred Years of the Smithsonian Institution; 1846-1946* (Washington, 1946). The life of the first secretary is given by W. F. Magie in the *Dictionary of American Biography* 8:552-53 (New York, 1932); by William B. Taylor, *A Memoir of Joseph Henry; A Sketch of His Scientific Work* (Philadelphia, 1879); and by Thomas Coulson, *Joseph Henry: His Life and Work* (Princeton, 1950), the latter vigorously defending him in his relations with Jewett. There is pertinent material relative to some of the principal figures of the early years in Samuel G. Brown, *The Life of Rufus Choate* (Boston, 1881); William H. Dall, *Spencer Fullerton Baird* (Philadelphia, 1915); and Richard W. Leopold, *Robert Dale Owen, A Biography* (Cambridge, 1940).

CHAPTER III

The most important sources of information on Jewett at the Smithsonian are his yearly reports and those of Joseph Henry in the *Annual Report*[s] *of the Board of Regents* for the years 1846 to 1855 (Washington, 1847-1856); Jewett's individual papers and publications; Cyrus Adler, "The Smithsonian Library," in G. B. Goode, *op. cit.;* and William D. Johnston, *History of the Library of Congress . . . 1800-1864* (Washington, 1904). The importance of his *Notices* is analyzed in Jesse H. Shera, "The Literature of American Library History," *Library Quarterly* 15:1-24 (1945). On exchanges the following are helpful: Elizabeth M. Richards, "Alexandre Vattemare and His System of International Exchange" (Unpublished MS thesis: Columbia University, 1934); an abridgment of the same in the Medical Library Association, *Bulletin* 32:413-48 (1944); and George H. Boehmer, *History of the Smithsonian Exchanges* (Washington, 1882).

CHAPTERS IV-V

Among the voluminous items discussing the stereotyping scheme and the rules for cataloging are Henry C. Bolton, "Bibliography," in G. B. Goode, *op. cit.;* Edward Edwards, *Memoirs of Libraries, Including a Handbook of Library Economy* (London, 1859) 2 vols.; A. Growell, "Some Notes on Co-operative or Labor-Saving Methods of Printing Library Catalogues—I," *Library Journal* 13:280-82 (1888); U. S. Bureau of Education, *Public Libraries in the United States; Their History, Condition, and Management, Special Report* (Washington, 1876); Samuel S. Green, *The Public Library Movement in the United States, 1853-1893* (Boston, 1913); U. S. Library of Congress, Descriptive Cataloging Division, *Cooperative Cataloging Manual for the Use of Contributing Libraries* (Washington, 1944); W. F. Poole, "Address of the President," *Library Journal* 11:199-201 (1886); John Fiske, "A Librarian's Work," in his *Complete Works* 8:313-49 (Boston, 1902); U. S. Library of Congress, *Annual Report of the Librarian . . . 1946* (Washington, 1947); and the introduction to Guido Biagi's translation of Jewett's 1853 work, *Della Compilazione dei Cataloghi per Biblioteche* (Firenze, 1888). The plates themselves have not been preserved at the Smithsonian Institution. The observations of a visitor to the Institution are given in Horatio S. White, *Willard Fiske, Life and Correspondence* (New York, 1925).

CHAPTER VI

S. S. Green, *op. cit.* has material on the convention of librarians in 1853, as does William I. Fletcher, *Public Libraries in America* (Boston, 1894), but the most complete account, based to a degree upon the papers of Seth Hastings Grant, is George B. Utley, "The Librarians' Conference of 1853; A Chapter in American Library History" (Unpublished MS: A. L. A.), which concludes that Jewett "did little toward actually working up the Convention," thereby correcting the impression given by Guild that Jewett was the prime mover. Jewett's opening address and other speeches are found in the Librarians' Convention of 1853, *Proceedings* (Cedar Rapids, 1915). See also L. Fagan, *The Life and Correspondence of Sir Anthony Panizzi* (Boston, 1881), 2 vols., concerning that librarian's disappointment in being unable to attend.

CHAPTERS VII-VIII

The unfortunate friction between Henry and Jewett is rehearsed at length by both antagonists in U. S. Congress, House, *Report on the Smithsonian Institution,* 33rd Congr., 2nd sess., H. Report 141 (Washington, 1855), and with even more one-sided vigor by Benjamin A. Gould in *Six Articles upon the Smithsonian Institution from the Boston Post, together with the Letters of Professors Peirce and Agassiz* (Boston, 1855). Charles Deane, "Memoir of George Livermore," Massachusetts Historical Society, *Proceedings* 10:415-68 (1867-1869) testifies to the aid that that gentleman gave Jewett in his struggles.

CHAPTER IX

The origin and early history of the Boston Public Library may be studied in the *Annual Report[s] of the Board of Trustees* from the year 1852, especially the preliminary report of 1852 and the reports for the years 1864, 1867, and 1877 (Boston, 1852-1877). Valuable, though varying in degree of detail, are Horace G. Wadlin, *The Public Library of the City of Boston, a History* (Boston, 1911); William W. Greenough, comp., "Annals of the Public Library of the City of Boston from the Year 1848 to its Removal to the New Edifice in Copley Square" (Unpublished work: Boston Public Library, n.d.); George Ticknor, *Life, Letters, and Journals* (Boston, 1876) 2 vols.; Justin Winsor, "Libraries in Boston," in his *Memorial History of Boston* (Boston, 1880-1881) 4 vols.; Carl L. Cannon, *American Book Collectors and Collecting, from Colonial Times to the Present* (New York, 1941); Jesse H. Shera, *Foundations of the Public Library; A Social History of the Public Library Movement in New England from 1629 to 1855* (Chicago, 1949); and Sidney Ditzion, *Arsenals of a Democratic Culture; A Social History of the American Public Library Movement in New England and the Middle States from 1850 to 1900* (Chicago, 1947). Jewett's labors are abundantly set forth in his yearly reports and those of the examining committees which are included in the annual reports of the trustees. Further light is shed by the manuscript records in the library, particularly the minutes of the trustees; Edward Everett, "Manuscript Notes to Mr. Jewett;" "Letters and Documents Relating to the Administration of the Library;" and

"Slips, Letters, etc. [Relating to the Administration of the Library]." The library also possesses two valuable scrapbooks, one on the Sunday-opening question and another of newspaper cuttings on the death of Jewett. The gathering of the Jewett family at Rowley is described and Charles Coffin Jewett's oration excerpted in the *Newburyport* [Mass.] *Herald,* June 19, 1855.

CHAPTER X

Allan Nevins, *The Ordeal of the Union* (New York, 1947) gives attention to the growth of libraries in the fifties.

CHAPTERS XI-XIII

The public library building is described in R. L. Midgley, *Sights in Boston and Suburbs, or Guide to the Stranger* (Boston, 1856); in clippings in Slips, Letters, etc. *(supra);* and, at a later date, in Justin Winsor, "The Boston Public Library," *Scribner's Monthly* 3:150-56 (1871). On book sizes, see Charles Evans, "The Sizes of Printed Books," *Library Journal* 1:58-61 (1876-1877), and Daniel Wight, "Book Sizes Again," *Library Journal* 5:177-78 (1880). On charging systems: Justin Winsor, "The Charging System at Harvard," *Library Journal* 3:338-39 (1878), which discusses the Boston Public Library system, as does Henry J. Carr, "Report on Charging Systems," *Library Journal* 14:203-14 (1889). S. Ditzion, *op. cit.,* treats of the Sunday-opening question and examines it more fully in his "Opening the People's Library on the Lord's Day," *School and Society* 70:49-53 (1949). The scrapbook on Jewett's death *(supra)* has material on his religious affiliations and descriptions of his last hours and character. A

181

photograph of Jewett may be found in H. G. Wadlin, *op. cit.*, and a cut of the same in J. Winsor, *Memorial History of Boston.*

182

Index

"Indicator," Jewett's, 152, 162, 170

Jackson, Andrew, 18-19
Jewett, John P., 4, 89, 93, 96, 133
Jewett family, 3, 15
attends reunion, 96, 113-14
Jillson, William E., 95, 129
Johnston, William D., quoted, 39, 86

Librarians, Association of, 73, 147, 171-72
Librarians' Convention of 1853, 51, 64-73, 97, 147, 170
Library manual, 72-3
Library of Congress
card, 171
catalog, 86, 95, 97-8, 101
Jewett's stereotyping plan for, 53-4, 58-60, 62-3, 170
Collection, growth of, 21, 34, 122, 163-64, 171
Jewett on, 81
Smithsonian Library transferred to, 97
Lincoln, Abraham, 148, 158
Livermore, George, 62, 67, 93, 113
letter from Jewett to, 89
in *North American Review*, 62
and stereotyping plan, 40, 51-3
Liverpool (England) Public Library, 72
Ludewig, Hermann, 35

McClellan, George B., 158
Manchester (England) Public Library, 72, 131, 152
Mann, Horace, 34
Marriage, 30

Marsh, George P., 22, 27, 76, 157
Mason, James M., 83
Mason Street building, 110-11
books moved to Boylston Street building, 118, 122-23
catalog of, 114, 117
Maury, John W., 83, 85, 100
Meacham, James, 59, 83, 87-8, 90, 93
Missionary work, Jewett considers, 5
Modern library movement, Jewett's effect on, 171-72
Mutilation of books, 148-49

National library, Jewett on, 80-1
New Bedford (Mass.) Public Library, 72
New York State Library, 137
Newspapers, quoted
on Jewett's resignation, 159
on Smithsonian Institution controversy, 61, 85, 89, 91-2, 94, 98
on Sunday opening, 138, 140
North American Review, 12, 21, 92, 162
Norton, Charles B., 64-5

Osgood, Samuel, 67, 72
Owen, Robert Dale, 22

Pamphlets, 143, 169
Panizzi, Anthony, 14, 44, 55, 65-6
Paris Municipal Council, 107
Parker, Theodore, 139, 161, 170
Patent Collection, 161
Pearce, James A., 58, 83
Peirce, Benjamin, 94
Peterborough (N.H.) Town Library, 72
Philadelphia, Library Company of, 34, 122, 142

186

Political Views, Jewett's 156-58
Polk, James K., 17, 22, 157
Poole, William Frederick, 66-7, 71
Poole's *Index*, 72, 126
Prescott, William H., 21
Prince, Thomas, 162; Library, 166
"Public libraries," Jewett's use of term, 33-4, 36
Public libraries, 72, 107-9, 121-22, 139, 170
Putnam's Magazine, 84

Quincy, Josiah, Jr., 108
Quincy schoolhouse, 115, 122

Religious beliefs, Jewett's, 5, 166, 139-40
Reuss, Jeremias David, 126
Rhees, William J., 36
Richards, Elizabeth M., quoted, 40
Rush, James, quoted, 142
Rush, Richard, 19, 83

Sabin, Joseph, 55, 172
Salaries, 10, 102, 120, 154-56, 159
Salem Latin School, Jewett at, 5
Seaver, Benjamin, 108-10
Shurtleff, Nathaniel, 109, 113, 164
Smith, Lloyd P., 67, 127
Smithson, James, 18, 22, 75, 104
Smithsonian Institution Library, 22-106, 164
Jewett at, 27-106, 169-70
Societies, Jewett's membership in, 6, 163
Sparks, Jared, 157
Stereotyping plan, 43, 45-60, 62-3 70-1, 86, 95, 97-8, 170-71
Cooley and others claim invention, 50-1

mechanical difficulties with, 54, 98
Stevens, Henry, 30, 40, 66, 98, 127
and stereotyping plan, 43
Story, Joseph, 161
Stuart, Moses, 5
Sunday opening, 137-40, 165

Tappen, Benjamin, 20
Taylor, H. R., 152
Taylor, Oliver Alden, 7, 11
Theft of books, 148-49
Ticknor, George, 21, 133, 164
and Jewett's *Index*, 123, 127-28
quoted, 109
work on Bates' booklists, 112-15
Totten, Joseph G., 83
Trinity Church, Boston, 167
Trumbell, Benjamin, 34
Tucker, William P., 143
Tyler, John S., 164

Uncle Tom's Cabin, John P. Jewett publisher of, 4
Union catalog, 28, 33, 43-4, 46, 171
Upham, Charles W., 93-5
Utley, George B., quoted, 65, 71
Uxbridge Academy, Jewett at, 5

Van Buren, Martin, 19
Vattemare, Alexandre, 38-40, 107
Vinton, Frederick, 129

Wadlin, Horace G., 152
Walker Tariff, 17
Wallace, John William, 67
Warren, Josiah, 49, 52-4
Wayland, Francis, 8, 19
Wilcox, Mr., electrotypist, 49
Winsor, Justin, 106, 125, 160, 166